Alex Bemrose was born in London and studied at Royal Holloway College, University of London, where she attained a BA Honours degree in History. She worked for four years in the ski industry, spending time living in the French Alps, followed by twenty-two years in corporate event management, running her own company for the last thirteen years, with clients in the financial sector including HSBC and Morgan Stanley. She closed the company after the arrival of her adopted son in order to be a full-time mother, and has since been involved in campaigning for changes to the adoption system. She lives on the outskirts of London with her husband, Dominic, and their son, José.

OUR SON FROM AFAR

The Long Road to Adoption

Alex Bemrose

Book Guild Publishing
Sussex, England

First published in Great Britain in 2010 by
The Book Guild Ltd
Pavilion View
19 New Road
Brighton, BN1 1UF

Typesetting in Garamond by
YHT Ltd, London

Printed in Great Britain by
CPI Antony Rowe

A catalogue record for this book is available from
The British Library.

ISBN 978 1 84624 674 6

Contents

Foreword   ix

Introduction   xiii

Part I: Research and Preparation (October 2005–March 2007)

1   'Trial by Jury'   3

2   The Journey Begins   8

3   Too White, Middle Class and Heterosexual   12

4   Back to the Drawing Board   28

5   Guatemala? Where's That?   35

6   Reality Dawns   40

7   Everything ... Including Your Inside Leg Measurement   47

8   Our First Taste of Guatemala   54

CONTENTS

Part II: The Waiting Game (April 2007–March 2008)

9	An Elephantine Gestation Period	75
10	We Have a Son ... a Son We Have Never Met	85
11	Politics Damn Politics	91
12	Meeting Our Son ... at Five Months Old	110
13	The Black Hole: Living in Limbo	123

Part III: Coming Home (April–July 2008)

14	The Final Stretch: Enough to Try the Patience of a Saint	167
15	Into Our Arms for Ever	178
16	Home at Last	184

Part IV: The Final Hurdle (July 2008–March 2009)

17	Readoption in the UK	191
18	Reflections	202

Epilogue	209
Postscript	211
Appendix 1: Timeline of Our Adoption Journey	215
Appendix 2: Abbreviations	219
Acknowledgements	221

Not flesh of my flesh,
Nor bone of my bone,
But still miraculously
My own.
Never forget
For a single minute,
You didn't grow under my heart,
But in it.

(Fleur Conkling Heyliger)

Foreword

This book is the moving, often heartbreaking account of the attempts by Alex Bemrose and her husband Dominic to adopt a child. Unable to have children of their own, they were determined to adopt. This is the story of the vicissitudes they encountered along the way, both in this country and abroad.

Adoption is a subject which, rightly and understandably, gives rise to strong emotions. It is also, in this country, riddled with political correctness.

I once made a speech in the House of Commons comparing the life chances of the many children in care to the much smaller number of those who are adopted. In it I told the story of another couple whose attempts to adopt had been thwarted at every turn. Afterwards I was accosted in the Tea Room by a Labour MP:

'There must have been something wrong with that couple,' she said. 'I should know. I used to be a social worker myself.'

I pointed out that the couple had actually been approved as suitable adoptive parents but even then had been defeated by the process. She was not persuaded.

The problems encountered by Alex and Dominic Bemrose when they tried to adopt in this country stemmed from the view that a child should be brought up in a family with parents of the same ethnicity as themselves. Clearly, in principle, this makes good sense.

But the majority of young children available for adoption in the UK are black, Asian or of mixed race. The majority of the couples wanting to adopt are white.

If that prevailing view were to continue, the prospects for a white British couple wishing to adopt a British child would be bleak.

And that is not the only obstacle. When Alex remonstrated with one of the many social workers she dealt with that it would be better if a mixed race or black child had a loving home with a white couple rather than being moved from one foster home to another, she received the following response:

'I'll tell you something,' the social worker replied, 'and don't say where you heard this. You and your husband have three large issues going against you. You are white, you are middle class and you are heterosexual.'

Worn down by these difficulties, Alex and Dominic decided to consider adopting abroad, having been dismayed, but paradoxically encouraged, by a broadcast on the *Today* programme featuring an interview with a woman from Manchester who had adopted a baby from China.

The woman recounted the following exchange with a social worker:

'Do I understand you correctly?' she had asked. 'I can go all the way to China, and adopt a little baby from Beijing, and you would assist me with my application and the process, but you would not allow me to adopt a little Chinese girl from Manchester?'

'That is correct,' the social worker confirmed.

So Alex and Dominic began to search abroad and, after considering many countries, settled on Guatemala, a troubled country bedevilled by the consequences of a long and bloody civil war, drug barons, armed gangs and crushing poverty.

Here again the bureaucratic obstacles were formidable, and, here again, there is an underlying reason.

Child trafficking is a serious international problem. It is easy to see how it could be disguised as international adoption. So checks and safeguards to ensure that the birth mother has freely decided to give up her baby are essential. The obstacles raised in Guatemala went far beyond that, however, and things seem to have got worse since this book was written.

But the story has a happy ending. Alex and Dominic have their little José and I would like to think that Alex will write a sequel in twenty years' time to tell us how he has grown up.

And, whatever else, do not miss the exquisitely appropriate poem by Fleur Conkling Heyliger at the very beginning of the book.

Michael Howard

Lord Howard of Lympne
Former Leader of the Conservative Party

Introduction

I hope this book, my 'Adoption Journal', will lead to a better understanding of the adoption system and the many problems with the adoption process in both England and overseas. There seem to be so many misconceptions about the process and I hope this will clarify at least some of them. It is an account of *my* personal experience and therefore gives my view of the process involved, and my understanding of the adoption systems in England and in Guatemala at the time of our adoption. As such it will, no doubt, differ from other adopters' experiences and views of the process. In short, it is my journey to motherhood and the emotions that I went through to get there.

This book is dedicated to my loving and supportive husband Dom, and to our wonderful son, José – a family at last. It is also dedicated to all the children throughout the world who are in need of a loving family and a home.

To those who are considering adopting a child: The road is very long and bumpy, but as Winston Churchill said in 1941, 'Never give in, never give in, never, never, never.' Have no doubt, it is so, so worth it when you reach the end of the road and hold that little bundle – *your* child – in your arms; a parent at last.

Note: *The names of all those connected with our adoption have been changed to protect their identities.*

Part I

Research and Preparation
(October 2005–March 2007)

1

'Trial by Jury'

Tuesday 27 March 2007

The wee small hours

I toss and turn. My heart is beating like a drum. I cannot sleep. Dom lies beside me, restless too. I know he is having as bad a night as I am having. Tomorrow – now today – is just about the most important day of our lives. Today we will be told if we can become parents; if we are eligible for adoption. Today we go before the adoption panel meeting. Seventeen months – so far – of research, preparation courses and interviews culminate in today's meeting. If we pass, we are eligible to adopt. If we fail, we are deemed unfit to adopt and bring up a child and our dreams die. It all hinges on today.

Dawn

As soon as it is light, I slip out of bed and head for the common opposite our house. It is a beautiful morning. A heavy blanket of fog hovers a few feet above the grass. The sun is low and glowing red in the early-morning light; the dew glistens on the grass. I walk quickly, trying to clear my head. I am in tears. Why oh why did our baby have to die? Why can we not just have a baby like everyone else? Why do we have to go through all this? All we want is to be parents ... Why oh why? Surely they cannot fail us, can they? We are just a normal couple. They fail some 'normal couples'. You never know. Will they, won't they? Will we, won't we? ...

3

'Get a grip, woman,' I say out loud, like some demented person holding a conversation with an imaginary friend. I look round quickly. Fortunately there is no one to hear me. I only see a few dog walkers in the distance.

I hasten back to the house, have a quick shower and throw on the carefully planned clothes for today's judgement meeting: a red cardigan, a sensible brown T-shirt, an A-line skirt with poppies on it and suitable low-heeled boots. I am trying not to look too smart, too middle class, too posh; I am trying to look like a mummy. Casual but with a hint of effort, and the red cardigan is a bit of a statement ... of what? I am not quite sure. *Power dressing*, I once heard it called. Perhaps it will give me confidence. Do I look right? I spend a ridiculous amount of time trying to decide on my underwear. The sexy black and red lacy bra and G-string is definitely not suitable. Might make me feel like a tart ... might show in my face. Dom appears in a pair of boxers. 'OK for today?' he enquires, laughing at my underwear indecision. 'Are my boxers suitable attire for a future father?' The moment is lightened – briefly.

Midday

We have just spent the most terrifying, intimidating half-hour of our lives. We had been warned in advance that sitting 'panel' was like taking your most important exam, going for your most sought-after job interview, and doing your driving test all rolled into one. Panel is the culmination of your adoption introductory meeting, the preparation course, and five months' worth of interviews with a social worker picking over every facet of your lives in nine three-hour interviews. It is the final stage in the process to become an eligible adopting parent, albeit only halfway through the entire adoption journey. The social worker prepares a lengthy document – the home-study report – based on her interviews with you both, on meetings with your referees, family, close friends, and past partners, and on a financial report, a medical report and a Criminal Reference Bureau report. Your lives to date are all documented in the most intimate detail in this home-study report, which is then sent to your panel judges – a group of appointed 'experts' who sit in judgement on your case. The panel is made up of representatives from all areas, including social workers, someone from the legal system, a doctor, someone who has been adopted, someone who has adopted, and a local councillor. They are playing the God-like role of making the decision as to whether you can become a parent or not. Your future is in their hands. Your dreams; your lives are in their hands.

We had been warned, but no one can prepare you for the complete feeling of helplessness, terror and intimidation. As you sit outside and await your summons, you know that behind that door those appointed experts already know just about everything there is to know about you. Today they have the opportunity to question you further on any areas which they feel are of concern before they put it to the vote: Are you eligible to adopt or not?

As we enter the room, we are met by a 'jury' of fourteen, seated expectantly round a boardroom table. They are smiling, trying to make us feel at ease. They have a job on their hands – we are terrified. We were told in advance they would discuss our case in front of us, but were warned that we could only speak when directly asked a question. It feels as if we are facing a murder trial ... and all we want is to become parents.

They start with questions about Guatemala, the country of our choice for adoption. We have just returned from a holiday there – timed so that our return would be just before our panel date and would hopefully impress our jury ... oops, Freudian slip ... panel ... who would thus understand our seriousness to adopt from Guatemala and our dedication to finding out about the country, the people and their culture.

They are obviously trying to commence gently. I feel relieved. The feeling is short-lived.

'Tell me, Dominic,' one of them asks, 'why a boy? You have put on your form that you want a boy. Why not a girl?' I know Dom is sweating. I can feel him visibly shrinking in his seat under the glare of fourteen pairs of eyes.

'I have always wanted a son. I suppose I am a traditionalist. I like the idea of carrying on the family name,' he starts.

'A girl can carry on the name,' one of our judges replies, obviously put out by his reply, which I can see she deems a sexist response. 'He may not like football, you know,' she continues.

'Nor do I!' Dom replies, trying to lighten the atmosphere.

'Oh yes,' I interrupt, despite knowing I should not speak unless spoken to, 'we are perfectly prepared that he may prefer ballet.' I desperately try to give the impression that we *are* the free-thinking, politically correct couple I know they think we should be. She is obviously not convinced. 'We will amend the form to "Boy preferred",' she says. It is not the moment to argue.

'Again, Dominic,' she adds, 'I see you were *sent*' – huge emphasis on the word 'sent' – 'I see you were *sent* to boarding school at a very early age. Can we be assured you would not do the same to your son?' Here we go again, I think, the anti-public-school brigade.

'Of course not,' Dom replies, becoming more forthright in his answers. 'It is unlikely we could afford private school anyway, but in the unlikely event that we could, maybe for A levels only. Certainly not before.' I can see he is making up lost ground. 'And only if it is suitable for our particular child. We wouldn't dream of it otherwise.' Fourteen heads nod in acknowledgement. Phew. Okay so far, I think. Ridiculous really. Should it not be our choice where we send our child to school? To boarding school even, if we so wish?

'Now Alex . . .' One of them starts on me. I feel the fourteen pairs of eyes swivel their gaze towards me. My heart is beating so loudly I can barely concentrate. I am intensely aware of the noise of a lawn-mower outside, competing with their voices. 'We notice you are blonde and blue-eyed,' she continues. What *is* coming next? Do I look too Aryan? Is she expecting a Nazi salute or something? Should I have dyed my hair brown? 'How do you feel about having a dark-skinned child? I mean, he will very obviously not be your birth child. He won't look like you, you know. Won't you mind?' What a daft question. Do they really think I have spent seventeen months

6

getting this far (a) without realising our child will not look like me, and (b) without wondering if I minded?

'I do realise he won't look like me,' I reply, stating the obvious, surely. 'I am prepared for and perfectly happy about the fact,' I continue, 'and think in a way it is a much more honest form of adoption. I mean, we will never have the quandary of whether or not to tell someone he is adopted. It will be obvious from the start.' The fourteen heads nod in agreement. Relief. I think my answer has satisfied them, in spite of my obviously unfortunate hair and eye colouring. I silently thank a friend who had responded similarly when asked the question in the same situation just a year previously.

More questions follow. They discuss a few details of our case.

'If you would like to wait in the room next door whilst we reach our decision,' the panel chairperson requests. We have been dismissed. They have to reach their decision over us. Oh my God ... Never has ten minutes seemed so long. We wait in the room next door. I feel like throwing up. Tears are pricking the back of my eyes. What is taking them so long? Didn't they like us? *Did they disapprove so strongly of my wish for a boy?* Dom thinks. *Am I too blonde?* I think. Irrationally we pick through their concerns and our answers.

'Congratulations.' The panel chairperson stands before us. 'We will be recommending you for adoption – a unanimous vote in your favour.' I want to kiss her. I want to kiss every one of them. I kiss my husband.

Alleluia! We feel like shouting from the rooftops. We are floating on air. Feel two stone lighter. The relief. The euphoria. We have passed. We are officially eligible to adopt. We *will* become parents. Our dream *will* become a reality.

We are excited and exhilarated – this will surely be one of the high points of our journey; a magical moment. Our dream of becoming parents is now that little bit closer.

2

The Journey Begins

14 October 2005: Seventeen months earlier

We have waited four months for this appointment. Today we are due to see one of the UK's leading baby doctors. Over the last six months we have been prodded and poked, investigated and analysed. We want a baby. We know there is nothing fundamentally wrong. We know it is just my age. I did get pregnant. We lost the baby. 'It is not easy to get pregnant at your age,' we are told again and again. 'Women like you, leaving it too late; putting career before family. Think you can then just get pregnant, just like that.' Why will they not understand? This was not the case. Not in my case anyway. How many other women echo these sentiments?

It is not always a lifestyle choice, leaving it so late. I had never intended to be a career woman. I had only ever wanted to be a wife and a mother, but sometimes life just is not that simple. My ex-husband had not wanted children. A fact I found out rather too late in the day. By the time our relationship was over and I was with Dom, I was more than forty years old. Not an age when pregnancy comes easy, I was to discover.

So here we were at one of London's leading fertility clinics eagerly awaiting our appointment with the great man himself. We were nervous but excited. I was trying to resist the temptation to believe he would just wave a magic wand and, *voilà*, I would be pregnant, but I could not help feeling optimistic. That was me – ever the optimist: when we had first tried for a baby, we found me wonderfully, magically pregnant within four months of trying, and when, just three months later the worst was confirmed – we had lost the baby – we desperately held on to the thought that I had managed to get pregnant so easily the first time round, so surely it would happen again. Our family are fertile stock, so my sisters always joke. Both of them only had to talk about getting pregnant and they conceived; my mother too. Yet they had all got pregnant in their twenties and thirties. It's a whole different ball game when you are over forty.

Our lives felt as if they were falling apart when I miscarried. I don't think I really truly realised how much I wanted a child until I got pregnant. It seemed the most wonderful thing in the world. I wanted to tell everyone. I just could not keep it a secret. I did not believe for one minute anything could go wrong ... ever the optimist.

We went through every possible emotion when we lost our much-loved, much-longed-for baby. We both wept as if our hearts were breaking. But if anything good came of it, instead of tearing us apart, it drew us closer together. When I was down, Dom was strong and cheered me up. When he felt low, somehow I found the strength to be strong for him. The grief kept surprising me ... a mother passing by with her buggy, a reference to the name we had called our baby, baby clothes hanging in the window of a shop ... and a wave of utter sadness would wash over me. I was dumbfounded that I could miss, in such a crippling manner, a being I had never seen. We planted a tree in the memory of our baby, swore never to forgot him – or her (how possibly could we?) – and we always mark the anniversary of his or her loss and birthday, the day he or she would have been born.

It is not so easy to get over the guilt though. If only I had not gone swimming that morning. If only I had not eaten that extra bar of chocolate the night before. There is no logic behind one's thoughts. The doctor had told me it just was not meant to be and not to go blaming ourselves, but you cannot help it. 'What sort of a mother am I,' I sobbed to Dom, 'if I couldn't keep my own baby alive?' 'I'm too old to be pregnant,' I'd cry. 'I never gave our poor baby a chance.' I am not sure the guilt and sorrow ever goes away, but it certainly lessens and becomes more manageable with time.

A year of potions and lotions followed. I tried every nature remedy, every 'hocus pocus' old wives' tale, and I eagerly read every book and article on the subject, in a vain attempt to get pregnant again. Chinese medicine, acupuncture, reflexology, yoga for relaxation, special diets, special supplements, homoeopathy – you name it; I tried it. I did not drink alcohol. I ate only healthy food. I became obsessed. I became stressed; stressed out beyond belief. No wonder I couldn't get pregnant again.

And so we commenced the round of tests only to find, as we already suspected, that there was no medical reason why I was not getting pregnant again. 'It's my ancient eggs,' I joked to Dom. But this was no joke. My age was surely the problem.

It is hard not to feel guilty when you cannot conceive. It is easy to feel a failure. Easy to start obsessing over thoughts such as 'I am not normal; not a real woman.' Easy to start resenting other women who fall pregnant so easily; easy to resent that young kid in the supermarket who looks barely out of school yet has two or three children in tow.

But to return to our appointment at the fertility clinic – one of the most distressing occasions of my life – Dom's too. The doctor had absolutely no sensitivity. Our personal concerns over the morality of *in vitro* fertilisation (IVF), of creating and then destroying embryos, with only two or three being implanted and the rest stored or destroyed, were met with a 'Well do you want a baby or not?' Our enquiries as to whether there was another course of action we could follow rather than IVF were met with a sales pitch for his clinic and a blunt refusal to discuss alternative routes. As far as he was concerned, IVF was our only chance. (I was not surprised to later read in the press that this same clinic was being investigated for malpractice, and for persuading women to go for expensive treatment that was either unnecessary or had little chance of success.)

Leaving it to nature, I had a three per cent chance of getting pregnant at my age, I was told. IVF would increase my chances to five per cent. IVF at his particular clinic would increase my chances to ten per cent. Still not great, I thought.

That may be the case, but having to sign a disclaimer before he even started to speak to us and his condescending tone and dismissive response to our enquiries felt quite appalling. He told me stress had nothing to do with my inability to get pregnant, said that he was likely to be able to solve the problem, that IVF was the obvious route. I should not worry over the embryos which would be destroyed, they were just cells.

That may have been his opinion; it was not ours.

I ran out in floods of tears, leaving poor Dom – as upset as I was at our treatment – to pick up the bill and follow me.

And so it was, over a glass of wine or two to calm us down at a nearby pub, that we decided enough was enough. No more desperate attempts to get pregnant. IVF was not right for us. We were going to go ahead and try to adopt a child instead.

3

Too White, Middle Class and Heterosexual

15 October 2005

Adoption had always been a strong possibility in our minds. We had talked about it from the time we first met. We planned that either we would have our own birth child and then adopt a second, or if we were not able to conceive, then we would adopt one or two children.

But where to begin? Google?

I type www.adoption.com on my laptop the next morning. I am met by a dozen, no, two dozen or more sites, all of them American. I try www.adoption.co.uk ... 'Adopt an endangered animal today', with a choice of adopting a rhino, an orang-utan or a snow leopard ... Umm ... Not exactly what I have in mind. Where do we start?

I stumble across a website for BAAF, the British Association for Adoption and Fostering, and find a list of agencies covering our area – seventeen in all. It's a start.

I can immediately cross out a few. 'We only accept applications from military families,' introduces one; 'We do not work with white adopters for young children,' says another. Is one allowed to specify such restrictions in this politically correct age? I ask myself. Little do I know, but I am soon to find out. Cross out; cross out; process of elimination, I think.

I start calling. 'We are a white couple,' I begin – I have quickly realised this is the first piece of information they require. 'We would like to adopt a baby or very young child or maybe siblings.' This is universally met with a torrent of denials about the likelihood of a baby being available. In an age where single motherhood no longer holds the stigma it used to and where terminations are so readily available, the majority of babies available are those which have been taken into care one, two or three years down the line when it has become obvious to social services that the mother, often on drugs or alcohol, can no longer cope.

I stumble across information on a Catholic adoption agency. 'We welcome people from all racial backgrounds; married couples; we have no upper age limit . . .' This looks more positive.

3 November 2005

Those poor kiddies; what an eye-opener. How terrifying. Last night we attended an 'Adoption Information Evening' run by one of the Catholic adoption agencies. Being a practising Catholic, I think this will be one box I can tick in our favour. It's a start.

How naïve could we have been? In my innocence, I just thought we could telephone an agency or our local council, be interviewed by social services to assure them we are 'good sorts', and then be given a child of the age we preferred. The child would of course have had a difficult start, but a bit of 'tender love and care' and all would be fine; happy ever after.

How naïve indeed. Oh dear, we have a lot to learn.

All children in the UK available for adoption are 'damaged'. This was the first point driven home to us at this meeting. How that word 'damaged' made me wince. They have *all* suffered neglect or abuse, emotional and/or physical. They will be difficult and untrusting, and quite probably will never get over the emotional and physical traumas they have suffered. Yes, you can help, but do not expect a miracle. Do not expect an easy ride. We will probably have to agree to maintain letter-box contact with one or other of the birth parents. Our child's birth parents will most likely be drug addicts or alcoholics. It will not be easy. And forget the idea of a baby, so few are available.

13

We learn that it is unlikely any agency will accept us unless we agree to adopt a child of at least three years of age, if not older. As a white couple we have even less chance of a baby or very young child. The social services like to give children to adoptive parents of the same ethnic background. There are very few white babies available; hence, it is very hard for white couples to adopt a baby. On and on they go. I wonder if they really do want adoptive parents. It seems as if they are doing all they can to put us off, and certainly none of the joys of having a family through adoption are mentioned.

Oh my God – this is scary. These problems are a little more than we have bargained for.

We still want to adopt though, and this has not put us off. Should we look overseas? I have read of people adopting babies from overseas. Will that be an easier route? Will that guarantee us a baby? A child less damaged by years of abuse or neglect simply because he or she will be that much younger?

It is all so confusing. Which is the best route for us? Where do we go for the information? Where do we start?

2 December 2005

Today we attended an 'Intercountry Adoption Consultation Day' – a full day's workshop to introduce PAPs (prospective adoptive parents) to the process of adopting a child from overseas.

Seven or eight couples, as nervous and, for the most part, as clueless as ourselves sit on the edge of their chairs. We all want to know the same thing. We are full of anticipation, hopeful that we will learn about the different countries we can adopt from and be given help with the daunting choice of which country. Not a bit of it, however.

'It is not politically correct to favour one country over another,' we are told. Today we will be given no information about the specific countries, just information on the process of adopting from overseas. Well that is all very well, but surely one of our first decisions must be 'which country'? It seems we will have to do this research ourselves. Where on earth do we begin? We are told that it is good if you have a certain connection with a country, an affinity towards the people and its culture. We will have to promote its culture, the country and its people to the child; take him or her back there to visit their native land, so it is important we choose a country with which we have an affinity or feel we can develop one with.

China is a popular country from which to adopt, but do we have an affinity with it? I know little about China except their 'one child' policy, which is the reason why so many children, and in particular baby girls, are available for adoption – and I also know that they have a terrible history of human-rights abuse. How could we promote that country to our child? Many prospective adopters are looking at Guatemala as it has a high level of poverty and hence there are many abandoned and relinquished children. We admit to knowing nothing about Guatemala. Russia? Another popular country, but the adoption laws are apparently set to change and we do not know when. Romania? It has recently closed its doors to international adoption, professing to have no problem with unwanted children and claiming to be perfectly able to cope with the situation at home. Africa? Are we prepared to deal with the risk of AIDS? And so we go on.

We play a board game, meant to illustrate the stages of the adoption process we will have to go through. It looks a bit like Monopoly and we are each given a different-coloured car. When I ask a question I am told my car is not in the square for asking questions. I have to land on a different box to be able to ask a question. This is ridiculous. We are not children. Can they not just explain the process? We are all adults here and just want information, not amusement with a child's game. Their endeavours to make the day more 'user friendly' and 'fun' just add to everyone's frustration. You can see it in everyone's faces but we are all too polite – or too scared of putting a foot wrong and falling at the first hurdle – to question the process.

When we are asked, at the end of the day, about our feelings on

15

the day and whether we found the board game useful, Dom replied, 'Where can we get hold of a copy for Christmas?' Everyone stifles a laugh. The social workers running the day are not amused. We fear a black mark has now been made against our application.

We leave, fed up and disillusioned. Why is it so hard to get started? Why is it so difficult to find out any proper information? Is there no one we can go to who can simply tell us the pros and cons of the various countries from where we can adopt?

We will have to do the research ourselves. We will have to look at every country individually and weigh up the pros and cons, check the regulations for adoption and whether we meet their criteria. No one is going to tell us the route we should take. We are going to have to find out for ourselves. Thank God for the Internet.

January/February 2006: Happy New Year!

Will this be the year we become a family? Will we have a child with whom to celebrate next Christmas and 2007?

We are full of determination to make a decision on which route we are taking, to sign with an agency and begin the process of bringing home a child. We realise now that it will not be easy, but we will not give up. There is no one to tell us where to go or how to go about it. Okay, we will find a way ourselves. I will dedicate half a day a week, a day if necessary, to doing the necessary research. I run my own company, organising corporate events, so I can allocate my own time, to a certain extent, though it will not be easy.

Back to the UK ... should charity not begin at home? We give up on the battle about which country we should adopt from by deciding to head back down the domestic adoption route. Why go abroad when there are so many children in this country in need of a good home?

I attend a council-run 'Adoption Information Evening' with my sister Kate for moral support, as Dom is away. There are about forty couples in the room, all of them white – well, this meeting was in

Twickenham, hardly the most ethnically diverse area of Greater London. 'We must warn you,' we are told, 'if all of you decide to sign up with us for adoption, we will only accept at most one third of you. We simply don't have sufficient white children available for so many white couples.' 'We need more couples from different ethnic backgrounds,' says another social worker. 'Don't worry,' Kate whispers in my ear. 'The rest are all heterosexual couples – they'll think we are a lesbian couple as we are the only two women who have come together. They'll hand us a child on the way out.' I cannot resist laughing at my sister's comment, which though being desperately politically incorrect, seems bizarrely to hit the mark. 'A single person or one partner of an unmarried couple – lesbian or gay – can adopt,' says the booklet I have been handed. I have already been told being white is a problem; perhaps being a heterosexual couple is a disadvantage too? No, surely not.

24 March 2006

It is a month since we sent our adoption application form to one of the Catholic adoption agencies that handles UK domestic adoptions, and we have been summoned to the first of two initial interviews. We are excited that at last we are properly beginning our journey to adopt. We have decided that as the process takes a while and as we would ultimately like two children, we will look into adopting siblings at the same time. This will give us a ready-made family at once and will hopefully make it easier for the children to adjust and attach to us if they have each other. We also hope that it will make us that little bit more attractive to the authorities and agencies and help speed up the process.

We have been speaking to a few friends and friends of friends who have adopted. It is amazing how they spring from the woodwork once you start looking. I didn't think I knew anyone who had adopted. Now I feel I know several. 'You have to tell them what they want to hear,' we are advised again and again. 'You'll have to appear totally politically correct' ... 'and not too middle class'. It seems strange that the social class we come from should be so relevant. Surely we just need to prove we can make good parents, I think. Why should our class or background be so relevant?

We are nervous but our two interviewing social workers try to put us at ease. One sits and takes notes – everything we say is recorded – while another asks us the questions. They are both friendly but inquisitive; incredibly inquisitive. I am amazed at the questions they ask. They tell us this is just an initial chat, for us to see if we wish to proceed with adoption, and if so, whether we wish to do so via their agency. It is also for them to see if we are indeed suitable adoptive parents. We are told that our backgrounds will be gone into in far more detail further down the line, and yet in just a couple of hours we already seem to have told them so much. They know about my family; that my father was an alcoholic, a point which seems to interest them intently ... I wonder if they are wanting to line me up with a child whose family has broken down due to alcoholism. They know I was previously married; that my ex-husband did not want children; they know my hobbies, my likes and my dislikes. They know about the job I do and about our quest for a child. They know we both went to boarding school. They know as much detail about Dom, too. How much more are we going to have to tell them before this process is over?

'Oh no, that wasn't a good answer,' says Dom as we leave the interview. 'I shouldn't have said my favourite hobby was rugby. That's far too middle class. I should have said I play darts instead.'

'Dreadful answer,' I agree, 'though not as bad as me telling them my favourite hobby was skiing. You can't get much more middle class than that.'

We joke, but underneath the banter we are concerned as to whether our answers were the right ones.

Concerned? Yes, but nevertheless we are confident that we will be asked back for the second interview. The social workers had told us it was helpful that we had been so open and honest. They were pleased at our desire for siblings. 'Are you sure you wouldn't like to adopt three children or more?' they had asked. 'We often have larger family groups needing placement. We would provide a car.' Three or four children? I thought, horror-stuck. Hold on a minute. We do not even know how to look after *one* yet ... And a car? What an extraordinary response. I laughed, thinking they must be joking, but no, their faces were deadly earnest. What a bizarre bargaining tactic – almost like some bargain-basement 'two for the price of one'-type offer. This is children we are talking about, not packets of biscuits. I knew Dom was echoing my thoughts.

They had shown an interest but obviously did not like the fact that we were public-school products, although Dom's comment that he was sent to the UK to boarding school from Singapore at age seven was met with an instant 'Ahh ... separation issues. Wonderful. You will understand about the issue of separation and rejection. You must have felt so rejected by your family.' I dared not look at Dom. What utter tosh. We may have been sent to boarding school young, but that does not mean we felt rejected by our families. Still, if that was what they needed to believe to deem us suitable – let them believe what they want. Equally keen on the fact that I was brought up in a family with an alcoholic parent, they obviously liked the fact that we had both 'suffered' in the past and therefore may be able to understand the problems experienced by so many of the children needing placement. I felt uncomfortable and disloyal having to talk about my father's problem with alcohol. I knew I couldn't hide it and had to be honest, but I felt it was no one else's business and felt very disloyal having to discuss it in detail.

They were not impressed at our lack of experience with young children. We need to do something about this – spend more time with our nephews and nieces and my godchildren. Find out how to look after young children. We need some experience. I have always shied away from spending too much time with my nephews and nieces and my friends' children, finding it painful when I wanted children myself so badly. I regret this now. I love my nephews and nieces and realise how much of their early childhood I have missed out on.

We are feeling a mixture of emotions tonight. We know the meeting went well and we felt an affinity with the social workers. We think they liked us and they were certainly impressed that we wanted to adopt siblings. They have already called us back for a second interview next month.

I enrol as a volunteer at a local primary school, helping out in the nursery class (three-year-olds) one morning a week for the summer term. I am neglecting my own business further, but this 'project' is so much more important. I know nothing of young children and feel I need some experience. I ring my sisters and offer to babysit.

We subscribe to the BAAF's newsletter *Be My Parent* – truly the saddest publication you could ever read. Page after page of photographs of young children, largely the offspring of drug addicts, alcoholics or child-beaters, staring out at you, with their most engaging smiles as they desperately implore you to give them a home. We feel uncomfortable looking at it. Is this how we will have to choose our child?

28 April 2006

Our second interview, and a different story this time: We now feel utterly confused. At the end of our first interview, we felt very positive. Now, after the second interview, we feel despondent and are wondering if we are indeed following the right route to adoption.

As soon as we met the social workers again, we were questioned about the length of time we have been together. We have only been married for just under two years, although we have known each other since 2002 and have been living together for almost three years. This appeared to be a problem for them. One of the requirements for adoption through this Catholic adoption agency is to have been married two years minimum before they can process an application. We were told that we may need to wait until July before we can progress further. Three months ... I suppose not a lifetime, but annoying nevertheless. We are impatient to move forward.

Of more concern was the question of the age of a child or children we can adopt. They started by querying whether it would be Dom or myself who would be the primary carer of the children. Who would stay at home and who would work? We are a traditional couple and this point has never been in question. Dom will continue working full time and I will become a stay-at-home mum initially and then perhaps return to work part time, after the child/children are settled or older (depending on the age we adopt). They did not seem satisfied with this answer. Would we consider it the other way round? I wondered what they were getting at. Did they think I wasn't suitable to care for children? It transpires that it was an age issue. I wondered when we would get to that. I am forty-four and Dom is thirteen years younger than me. Although we had initially been told that age was not an issue these days, in reality it appeared it could still be a barrier to adoption.

They were aware we wished to adopt siblings as young as possible, but . . . and now they got to the crux of the matter: the majority of young children available for adoption in the UK are black, Asian or of mixed race; the majority of couples wanting to adopt are white. Most couples want to adopt a child or children as young as possible. The current guidelines followed by the local authorities in the UK are that a child should be brought up in a family with parents of the same ethnicity as themselves. Hence there is a problem. There are many children – young children, babies even – available for adoption, but they are, in the main, not white, and therefore the precious few white young children available for adoption will go to the younger adoptive parents.

It would help our quest for a younger family if Dom became the primary carer and I worked full time. No, we would not do that. We would not change the way we wished to bring up our children just because of their ridiculous rules. I may be thirteen years older than my husband but I am fitter and more active and perfectly capable of looking after young children. I am aged forty-four, not eighty-four. Why should my age be an issue?

Dom agreed (fortunately), and we arrived at an impasse with the agency. The result? As the interview progressed we were pressurised further and further from our desire for a young family towards older siblings. Not only that, but also towards children who have additional special needs.

Now, don't get me wrong here. These children need a home. I am full of admiration for couples or individuals who adopt an older child or children, and/or children with additional mental or physical disabilities. However, these special needs are going to be on top of the additional special needs the child will already have, as a result of the experiences he or she will have suffered in early life. We just do not feel able to take that on. Not when we have no experience of children in the first place. They were very interested in the fact that one of my nephews is on the autistic spectrum and that I enjoyed being in his company. I can see that they are hinting at this experience being useful if we were to adopt an autistic child.

I feel we are being steered away from what we want. We want to bring up a child or children from the start; from babyhood, or, failing that, from a year or so old. We do not want to adopt a child who is already halfway through his childhood and we do not feel that, as first-time parents, we could cope with a child with additional special needs.

We leave the meeting feeling depressed. They are going to discuss our case with the committee but declare that they feel we would be best suited to adopt siblings aged seven or eight or older, with at least one of them with additional special needs.

We are, however, advised that there is one other route we could investigate. As there are so few younger white children available for adoption, it may be easier for us to adopt one if we go directly through a local council rather than through an agency. The children who this Catholic agency has for adoption are referred to it from the various local councils, so whilst we thought the agency route would give us access to a wider group of children (i.e. from all over the UK rather than just from the area in which we live), we are told that the downside is that the children who are easiest to place (that is, the younger white ones) will already have been immediately placed by the local councils before the agencies get a look in.

May 2006

A frustrating few weeks. I have now rung every local authority from which we would be eligible to adopt, based on where we live. I have contacted the Adoption and Fostering Department of each of these authorities. It is a laborious task. On succeeding in getting through the phone system to the right person, one then has to go through twenty questions or more from the social worker before any information can be disclosed. It takes me the best part of a week – oh, how my business is being neglected – to cover the seven or eight authorities in our area.

Their responses are quite unbelievable.

I try the first one – the town next to the one in which we live. 'You live too close,' I am told. 'We wouldn't want to place our children at a location so close to where they originally have come from.' I try the county next to ours. 'Sorry, you are not in our area,' I am told. 'Too far.' This is now beginning to get ridiculous.

I ring our local authority. 'What ethnicity are you?' is their first question. 'White,' I reply, taken aback that once again this should be the first, and therefore presumably their most relevant, query. 'Oh, I'm so sorry,' the social worker replies, 'we are not accepting any more white couples, not for the moment anyway.' My jaw hits the floor. Is one even allowed to utter such prejudices in this politically correct era? 'Such a shame you are not black,' she continues. 'We have a wonderful little black baby girl we are looking to place.' 'Black is fine,' I reply, suddenly hopeful. 'We'd be very happy with a little black baby.' 'Oh goodness me no, we certainly couldn't place a little black girl with a white couple,' I am told.

I still find it hard to get my head around the fact that we apparently have to seek a young *white* child; that the colour should be so important, so relevant. We do not care about the colour of the

23

child, and if there are so many more black, Asian or mixed-race children needing homes, then why cannot we be considered for one of them? I find the current UK policy extraordinary. Surely it is political correctness gone crazy?

I call another neighbouring council. 'I am so sorry,' I am politely told. 'You see ... umm ...' She is obviously having difficulty spitting out our rejection. 'You see ... I'm afraid we can't take any more white couples onto our books.'

I continue calling – four, five, six, seven more local authorities ... it is all the same story. 'We might be able to accept you on our books for an older child,' I am told, 'but certainly not for a baby or a young child. It is your ethnicity, you see.' It is my first experience of racism; I feel we are being discriminated against for our colour. It is a novel experience.

In desperation I pour my heart out to one of the rather more sympathetic-sounding social workers. 'I would understand it,' I say, 'if there were lots of ethnically diverse couples wanting to adopt. If you had a little Jamaican baby available for adoption and there was a black couple ready to adopt and ourselves, all things being equal, give the child to the black couple. Obviously this would be easier for him growing up. But surely if there aren't enough mixed-race or black couples wanting to adopt, wouldn't it be better the child had a home with us, a white couple, than spent its childhood being moved from one foster home to another?'

'I'll tell you something,' she replies softly, 'and don't say where you heard this, but I like you so I am going to be completely honest ... You and your husband are going to face a tough time if you are to be accepted to adopt domestically. You have three large issues going against you ...' I wonder what these could be. My age? No. 'You are white, middle class and a heterosexual couple,' she states bluntly. Stunned, I hang up the phone. Has the world gone completely mad?

It appears that the facts are as follows: The current guidelines followed by the local authorities in the UK are that children should be brought up by parents of the same ethnicity as themselves. In an ideal world I would agree that this is best; however, there are

24

considerably more mixed-race, black and Asian children needing homes than there are mixed-race, black and Asian couples wanting to adopt. The result? For the year ending 31 March 2006, there were approximately 60,300 children in foster care in the UK. In the same year 3,700 children were adopted domestically, a three per cent decrease on the number adopted the year before. What happens to the rest? Well, a few go back to their families, but a large number are moved from foster home to foster home, children's home to children's home, and never experience a permanent family and a stable upbringing.

Not only is there a shortage of suitable candidates of the right ethnicity – that is, of the same ethnicity as the children – to provide permanent adoptive homes to the children in our care system, but there is also a desperate shortage of foster homes. Seventy per cent of children in the care system are looked after by foster parents, but there is currently a shortage of 10,000 foster carers.

'Looked-after' children are five times as likely to suffer mental health problems, eight times more likely to be permanently excluded from school, and, aged ten years or older, are more than twice as likely as other children to have received a conviction. No wonder there are so many troubled souls out there. Surely there should be a time limit – that is to say, if a home has not been found for a child with adoptive parents of the same ethnicity within a certain amount of time, then parents of other ethnicities should are considered.

We have been turned down; rejected because of our colour. Dom blows a gasket when he gets home. He is not a violent man by nature, nor does he have a bad temper, but this has really got to him. He bangs his fist on the table and stamps his feet. 'If we were black and they'd said that,' he replies to my comment that that so many local authorities had turned us down because of our colour, 'we would have had them in court.' He certainly has a point.

It is not only our ethnicity that is a problem, our desire to adopt a baby or young child is also a sticking point. Most PAPs (prospective adoptive parents) want to adopt younger children. It is understandable. They have had fewer years of disruption and, in many cases, abuse, and therefore find it easier to settle in their adoptive home. Furthermore, the majority of couples wishing to adopt want to bring up a child from the start of its life, rather than taking on a child halfway through his or her childhood. Of the 60,300 children in care in the UK, 49,000 are under sixteen years of age and there are plenty of much younger children and babies in the care system, but there is not a sufficient number of *white* babies and young children in the system eligible for adoption to fill the demand of *white* couples wishing to adopt.

Another contributory factor to the high number of children still looking for adoptive homes in this country is the fact that a lot of them need very specialist care. They have been badly damaged by their early experiences and if you are first-time parents, you may not be the most suitable parents for them.

There is, however, so much that I think is wrong with the UK system for adoption. In an effort to be politically correct the pendulum seems to have swung too far and it does not look like swinging back to a neutral position – not in the foreseeable future, anyway. There seems to be a set of blanket rules that all the social workers apply without intelligently and flexibly weighing up an individual or an individual couple and seeing what they could offer as parents. The incompetence of the system; the absence of intelligent consideration of couples who could offer children a good home, and the strict adherence to the set of rules that have been put in place mean that thousands of children remain in care, whilst couples who could offer good homes either give up or look overseas for a child, just because they do not fit the ideal in terms of age or ethnicity. I wonder how many couples and individuals have been turned away or put off by the system. It is very sad. Ultimately it is the children still looking for permanent homes who suffer.

June 2006

A month later we get a response from the Catholic adoption agency to which we had applied. We are approved to continue on to the next stage ... providing we are happy to go with their recommendation that we may be potentially suitable as adoptive parents for siblings aged seven or eight years or older and maybe with additional special needs.

Unless we are prepared to accept such a child or children, they will not continue to process our application.

We politely decline.

4

Back to the Drawing Board

May/June 2006

We will not be beaten. There must be a way to have a family. We will not give up.

So, we have been rejected from the UK system (unless we wish to adopt a much older child). The rumours were right. We had been warned. It is not easy to adopt within this country, particularly if you want a very young child. We need to look overseas. Dom and I go round and round in circles, discussing it night after night. We want a family. We will have family. We will find a way.

We contact our local authority once more. 'We are interested in adopting from overseas,' I begin. We are interviewed once more, this time with a view to ICA (intercountry adoption).

As with the interviews we had for domestic adoption, the social worker focuses on the problems and negative issues surrounding adoption. Social services, it seems, does its level best to put one off adoption, be it domestic or intercountry. There is little recognition of the joy one will, no doubt, experience at the end of the journey with a child of one's own, and instead only a focus on the negative aspects. This must put off so many people. Is it any wonder that currently less than five per cent of children in care in this country are ever found a permanent home? That figure is absolutely scandalous.

Dom and I find it a little strange that social services do not consider our ethnicity (i.e. the fact that we are white) a problem for ICA, even though it was a problem for domestic adoption. The same local authority who will not place a British child with parents of a different ethnicity from his or her own are quite happy to assist with – and indeed condone – adoption from overseas, where the child will clearly not only be of a different race and probably colour but will also have spent his or her earliest years in a completely different part of the world being brought up in a different culture.

Does that not strike you as rather hypocritical?

In addition, of course, we have to pay for this privilege. The cynic in me cannot help noticing that whilst no local authority receives payment from adoptive parents wishing to adopt domestically, if you wish to adopt internationally you have to pay your local authority several thousand pounds to process your application ... I will say no more.

A few months later the reality of the UK policy on adoption would be neatly summed up for me by an adoptive parent on Radio 4's *Today* programme. A well-spoken woman interviewed from her home in Manchester spoke of her experience and what led her to adopt from China. She and her husband had tried for many years to have a child and failed. They wanted to adopt a baby girl and rang their local authority. They were hopeful, and aware that they lived in an ethnically diverse area, were quick to add that they did not mind the race or colour of the child they adopted. They were interviewed by a social worker who brought up the issue of their colour (white) and their social standing (middle class). She felt they would be *better suited* to look internationally for a baby – perhaps from China. 'Do I understand you correctly?' the woman replied. 'I can go all the way to China, and adopt a little baby girl from Beijing, and you would assist me with my application and the process, but you would not allow me to adopt a little Chinese girl from Manchester?' 'That is correct,' the social worker confirmed.

It beggars belief. This country really has gone stark raving mad.

So, from which country should we adopt? I start my research again.

China – lots of deserted babies; Romania – dreadful film footage

29

of children abandoned and unloved left in cots in dreadful conditions; Africa – orphans from AIDS and from war-torn countries; Russia – visions of babies left in cots in orphanages and rumours of unreliable medical reports; Thailand, Vietnam, Guatemala, Poland, Nepal, India, South America, the USA, Sri Lanka ... the list of countries from where one can adopt seems endless. So many children needing homes; so many tragic, heartbreaking situations, but where does one begin? How does one choose? They all have children in desperate need of parents and good homes. How can one make that choice?

Back on the Internet, I soon realise that this is going to be a lengthy process. Without a natural *connection* with a particular country, we will have to individually look at each country and see whether we feel it is the 'right' country for us to adopt from. The problem is that we do not really mind where our child comes from and we do not have a natural draw towards any particular country. We do need to be careful. We have heard terrible stories of people being drawn inadvertently into child trafficking; of couples turning up at orphanages to find the child they have been 'referred' (offered or matched with) is terribly ill or suffering from some terminal illness or disability about which they had not been informed; of agencies taking their money with promises of a child and then disappearing into thin air.

We need to do this properly – legally and carefully – for us and for our future child. We want to ensure that we minimise our risk of disappointment – that is, of never getting the child, of the child being so ill, traumatised or disabled that we are unable to cope, or of finding that it puts too much of a strain on us and our relationship – not good for us or our child, and obviously, we certainly do not want to get involved in a child-trafficking situation.

We keep hearing about China. So many people seem to be adopting from there. Perhaps we should consider it? We decide against it. We would have a problem promoting the country and its culture to our child, when the system has such an appalling human-rights record. Furthermore, we have decided to adopt a baby boy

(Dom really wants a boy and I am happy with either), but due to their 'one child' policy, and because boys are deemed more desirable for labour purposes, most abandoned babies in China are little girls.

Guatemala is a country mentioned to us, a country in need of adoptive parents. I do not know anything about Guatemala, however, so we put that one on hold for the moment whilst we look at the countries that we know a little more – or at least something – about.

We decide against Russia. We hear that the adoption laws are due to be revised some time soon, and who knows when? Just our luck, we would be halfway through the process and then back to square one when a new set of laws are instigated. Furthermore, we watch a heartbreaking television documentary about a couple going to Russia with no clear ideas of the sickness the child they are to adopt is suffering from. The orphanage is clearly trying to cover up the real problems. The translator is obviously not translating the responses from the doctor to them in full. They take the poor little mite back to their hotel room. He is covered in sores and dies that night. They are heartbroken. The process, it is clear from that programme, is so full of risks. It seems there are a lot of dishonest people involved. In addition, alcoholism is such a problem in the country that so many of the children suffer from foetal alcohol syndrome. It is one more problem to add to the list of potential problems the child will arrive with. It is an additional problem we feel unable to face.

Romania has currently closed its doors to international adoption, professing not to have a problem regarding the welfare of its children and saying that it is able to look after its abandoned children domestically. The rest of the world knows this is not the true picture and that the state of many of their orphanages is still dire, but we are unable to adopt from Romania at the moment, so end of story, as far as our plans to adopt are concerned, at least.

Adoptions from Cambodia into the UK have been suspended since 2004 due to concerns over their adoption process.

We look into Singapore. Dom spent his childhood up to the age of twelve in Singapore, and thus has quite a connection to the place. His family, too, would be able to provide any child we adopted from there with information on the people and customs of the country as he was growing up. 'Must be a resident for a minimum of six months,' I read in the list of criteria for PAPs. Sadly, we are not in a position where we can just abandon our jobs and go and live somewhere else for six months.

We consider Poland. My grandmother is Polish and I grew up hearing the legends and history of our family and the country of Poland. Although only part Polish myself, I definitely feel I have a connection there, and Dom is as happy for us to adopt from Poland as from anywhere else. More research ... We are unable to adopt from Poland. The regulations state that you must speak fluent Polish (I know none); at least one of you must live in the country for a minimum of three months prior to adopting there (not possible with either of our jobs, and we are not prepared to be apart for three months); in addition, we have to prove we follow Polish customs within the household (well, we do follow one particular Polish custom of breaking and sharing bread each Christmas – a custom which leaves Dom and my brother-in-laws totally confused and perplexed); and ... and yes, maximum age for adoptive parents is forty years old. We do not meet their criteria, so Poland is out.

Sri Lanka? Lovely people; poor country. There is a five-year waiting list after your adoption application is accepted before you can proceed with the adoption ... We are not waiting that long.

Nepal? This has been at the back of our minds for a while. Dom's father was in the Gurkhas and even speaks Gurkhali. The Nepali people have always struck me as a wonderful race. They have a reputation as being friendly, loyal and beautiful. I have an almost obsessive love of the mountains and can just picture us trekking through the mountains to show our son his birthplace ... perhaps a chance to visit Everest base camp – a long-standing ambition of mine. I know I am getting carried away romancing about it, but ... yes, I rather like the idea of bringing up a child from Nepal.

I email the British embassy in Nepal and the Embassy of Nepal in London. I am not sure if this is the right route, but it seems a good place to start.

Two weeks later, out of the blue, I receive an email from an old friend of mine, Clare, who lives in Spain: The email is titled 'Our son from Kathmandu'. I can hardly believe it. She and her husband are adopting a four-year-old from Nepal. What a coincidence. I email back to hear their story. They have just returned from meeting their son in the orphanage that has been his home for the last four years. They are now back in Madrid awaiting the completion of the paperwork before they can go back out and collect him. This orphanage seems better than many – cleaner and with a reasonable reputation for honest reports and good practices. I email the director and receive a polite and charming response. He would be happy to assist with our adoption from Nepal once we have passed the adoption panel and our documents are ready, providing we meet with the Nepali criteria for adoption. Oops ... forgot to check that. Meanwhile I get a response from the British Embassy in Nepal. It does not tell me a lot.

I finally track down the list of criteria for potential adopters from Nepal. We need to be married for four years before we can com-mence the process and also will require a letter confirming my infertility from our doctor. I go and visit our doctor. No, she will not sign a letter confirming my infertility. I have been pregnant and therefore could get pregnant again. 'You see,' she explains slowly and patiently, as if I am a child being told the facts of life, 'until you have reached the menopause, there is a chance of pregnancy.' How frustrating. I cannot seem to get pregnant again, but because I have been pregnant in the past we cannot adopt from Nepal.

This seems very odd. A single woman can adopt from Nepal just like that, but if you are married you need to have been married for a minimum of four years and need to prove your infertility. Are they presuming a single woman would never get pregnant? It is yet another example of the strange and inexplicable rules and regula-tions of the adoption process.

Where next? Thailand? I read that the current waiting list is eighteen months and likely to get longer. Forget that one then.

'I wouldn't mind holidaying in Mauritius,' Dom says one evening.

Fine, let's look at Mauritius then. For want of a better reason, I suppose a desire to holiday in the country of our choice could be as good a one as any. One of Dom's best friends is from Mauritius – another reason for our choice? I check the criteria. It looks possible. I am told that all arrangements need to be channelled through the embassy. I email the British embassy in Mauritius. No answer. I fax the embassy. No reply. I telephone. The phone just rings and rings. I fax again. I email again. Two weeks later and I still cannot get a response. I send a letter by special delivery. 'Please can someone give us some information on the possibility of adopting a young child from your country?' I never hear back. Some time later I am told that whilst the official list of regulations advises that Mauritius is open to overseas adoption, in reality it is virtually impossible to adopt from the country unless you are a native of Mauritius. Forget Mauritius then.

I go and see my parish priest. Does his order (which is a missionary order) have connections with any orphanages in the world? Can he help? He is sympathetic to my request but unable to assist with my enquiries.

It sounds like we are being flippant over our choice of country. This really is not the case, but without help and direction, without an obvious country to approach, and with so many children in so many parts of the world in need of a home, it is hard to know which way to turn. We feel like we are going round in circles, waiting for I know not what – a flash of inspiration? A sudden draw to a country? Someone or something to point us in the right direction?

5

Guatemala? Where's That?

June 2006

I can't remember whether it is Dom or I who first mentions that we should consider adopting from Guatemala. I don't know why it takes us so long to get round to considering this country, a country which turns out to be absolutely the perfect choice.

Guatemala has previously been recommended to us, but knowing nothing about the place, we have passed over it without further discussion. I am embarrassed to admit that I am not even quite sure where Guatemala is – is it South or Central America? Is it an island or on the mainland?

Back to the Internet ...

Guatemala: A country of striking features and a strong indigenous culture, Guatemala's natural beauty and powerful identity stand in stark contrast to its bloody past and troubled present. Mountainous, heavily forested and dotted with Mayan ruins, lakes, volcanoes, orchids and exotic birds, Guatemala is one of the most beautiful countries in Central America ...

Sounds idyllic ... but I read on:

In 1996 the country emerged from a 36-year-long civil war which pitted leftist, mostly Mayan insurgents against the army, which – backed by the US – waged a vicious campaign to eliminate the guerrillas. More than 200,000 people – most of them civilians –

were killed or disappeared. Despite an official finding that 93% of all atrocities carried out during the war had been committed by the security forces, moves to bring those responsible to account started only after a long delay. Guatemalans live in one of the most inequitable societies. Poverty is particularly widespread in the countryside and among indigenous communities. Illiteracy, infant mortality and malnutrition are among the highest in the region, life expectancy is among the lowest, and in common with many of its neighbours, the country is plagued by organised crime, drug-trafficking and violent street gangs. (www.news.bbc.co.uk)

I 'Google' more facts on the country: Guatemala is a constitutional democratic republic; approximately 50 to 60 per cent of the population are Maya (also known as Mayan), the indigenous people of Guatemala, and the rest are Ladinos (largely descendents of both the Maya and the Spanish who conquered the country in the sixteenth century); 60 per cent of the population speak Spanish and the remaining 40 per cent speak more than twenty different Maya Indian languages; 50 per cent of the labour force are involved in agriculture (mainly sugar cane, corn, bananas, coffee and beans) and 15 per cent work in industry (mainly sugar, textiles and clothing).

Further research leads me to more relevant information regarding the poverty level and the plight of the children of this country. I read that Guatemala is one of the poorest countries in the Americas, with 57 per cent of the population – 78 per cent of the indigenous population – living below the poverty line and a huge 90 per cent of the population having no access to any medical care. UNICEF reports that 67 per cent of indigenous children suffer from chronic malnutrition, that infant mortality is at 40 per 1,000 live births (46 per 1,000 live births for indigenous children, and double this figure in isolated rural indigenous areas), and also that maternal mortality in childbirth is very high too. These levels of chronic malnutrition are much higher in Guatemala than in any other country in the Latin American and Caribbean region, and contribute to stunted growth and severely compromised immune systems.

Furthermore, schooling is deficient in many areas – one fifth of children aged seven to fourteen are currently working, and 44.5 per cent of the population (77 per cent of the indigenous population) are illiterate.

There are no official statistics on the number of street children in Guatemala, but in its 2000 report to the United Nations Committee on the Rights of the Child, the government of Guatemala estimated that there were between 3,500 and 5,000 street children in the country. Other reports give figures that are double or even treble this number. Yet another 25,000 to 30,000 live in orphanages, mostly private.

Many of these children have been orphaned by civil war and violence; some are runaways from physical or sexual violence – sexual abuse and incest affects 30 per cent of girls and 18 per cent of boys – and a large number are relinquished or abandoned by parents, too poor to cope.

On the streets, children soon fall prey to violence, exploitation and disease. They are rejected by society and known as 'disposable'. (How can any child possibly be referred to as 'disposable'? I shudder to think.) They become victims of harassment and violent abuse. Some are shot by police. Many children seek to numb the pain and loneliness by turning to solvent abuse. At high risk, 408 children were killed in the first ten months of 2002 alone (an increase of 27 per cent from 2001); some were killed by gangs, others by security forces, and others in drive-by shootings. Guatemalan street children have also been killed in extrajudicial executions.

In only a few days on the streets, children as young as four or five learn to dodge the threat of violence from passers-by, the batons of the police, vigilante bullets and the predators running prostitution rings. They soon learn that survival depends on constant scavenging for food (or simply ignoring sickness and hunger), finding secret places to sleep, and the camaraderie of the 'gang'. They beg, they rob and they turn to drugs and prostitution, purely to survive. (Children account for 80 per cent of the prostitute population in Guatemala.) Toybox, a charity working with the street children of Latin America, estimates that the life expectancy of a street child in Guatemala is approximately four years.

The government of Guatemala has not put any money into a social welfare programme, so there is no infrastructure to care for the homeless children in their own country. As there is virtually no domestic adoption, intercountry adoption is the only viable option for the healthy survival of many of these children.

According to ICA statistics issued by the US Department of State, between 3,500 and 4,500 Guatemalan children a year are currently finding homes in the United States through the legal intercountry adoption process. An additional number – less than one thousand – are adopted from Guatemala into other countries around the world.

The more we read the more intrigued we become and the more drawn we feel to Guatemala. This is a country with children in need of help.

A check with the Intercountry Adoption Centre confirms that we do indeed fall within the necessary regulations and requirements for adopting from Guatemala. Further research reveals that the country appears to be a tried and tested route for intercountry adoptions, with a legal system in place for adoptions from Guatemala to the United States and, to a lesser extent, to the UK. Adoption statistics published in 2006 by the UK Department for Education & Services (now known as the Department for Children, Schools and Families [DCSF]), which receives approximately 350 applications a year for intercountry adoption, indicate that from 2000 to 2006, 146 applications were received to adopt from Guatemala. This total was surpassed only by adoption applications for China (currently the most popular country for intercountry adoptions), with 1,003 applications, for Russia, with 172, and for India, with 148.

Considerable further research reveals that there are a number of adoption agencies – all American based – that can arrange adoptions from Guatemala to England. There are even two support groups in England (Guatemalan Families Association and Guatemalafeliz) for families who have adopted from Guatemala or who are in the process of adopting from the country. I speak to a few of the adoption agencies. Their responses are positive. The majority of the children in Guatemala available for adoption are relinquished by women who are either unable to cope with another mouth to feed or, if single, unable to find a way to care for their child and at the same time work in order to earn food to live. It is tragic, but many women see the act of relinquishing their child(ren) as the only way to ensure their future survival. One of the attractions of adoption from Guatemala is the care that the children receive prior to adoption. Many are fostered by families (at the cost of the adoptive parent(s) who have accepted the referral to adopt the child) rather than staying in orphanages, and they are therefore likely to get more individual care and attention. The foster families vary in quality, of course, but this is so much better for the development of children and is one of the deciding factors for many who decide to adopt from this country.

Wonderful. Decision made. Guatemala it is. We feel immense relief at having finally reached a decision; another hurdle overcome.

We find a postcard of a little Guatemalan baby boy, dressed in national costume. He looks very cute. I put the card on a shelf in the kitchen where we can see it when we sit at the table to eat. We give him a name – José – and focus on him when we discuss our adoption.

This name was picked for no particular reason; we chose it simply because it is a Spanish name and they speak Spanish in Guatemala and we just like the sound of the name 'José'. We will call our son-to-be 'José' until we find out exactly who he is, and then we will probably change it to the name he has already been given. That is, providing it is not 'Jesus'. Jesus is a common name in Guatemala, but I would feel I was blaspheming every time I told off a child called Jesus.

Some time soon, I hope, the picture on our kitchen shelf will be replaced by a photograph of our real life 'José', the son who we will be bringing home. We cannot wait.

6

Reality Dawns

July/August 2006

Intercountry Adoption Preparation Course
... the aims of the preparation course are both to inform and enable you as prospective adopters to develop ideas and skills to bring to adoptive family life ... expectation ... work prior to attending the first day ... work in between the sessions ... preparatory reading ...

Another box to be ticked, we think. We have to go through the motions. Show willing to jump through all the hoops. Such old cynics that we are, we did not really think it would actually provide us with anything useful. We have been proved so wrong.

The Intercountry Adoption Preparation Course has proved a revelation; a fascinating, if somewhat alarming, insight into 'what to expect', an education, and a network of friends and support for the future. Everything it had said it would be and everything we cynically believed it was not likely to be.

It brings home to us the reality of what adoption really means, how long the journey will be, and just how much further research and preparation we need to do.

The course is an integral part of our preparation to become adoptive parents. A report will be written on our involvement in the course and this will be included in our home study, which will be prepared by our social worker after a series of interviews. The home study will then be put before a panel of 'judges' to vote on our eligibility to be adoptive parents.

The course consists of three full-day sessions over a month in a room at a local council office in Clapham. It is stiflingly hot – we are in the midst of a heat wave – and emotionally draining, but a thoroughly useful exercise.

There are ten couples, including Dom and me, on the course. We are all slightly nervous but full of anticipation and excitement about the future and about another hurdle being overcome. We are all anxious not to put a foot wrong, to appear interested and willing to learn, as indeed we are.

We are given homework after each session, to be completed before the next. There is a questionnaire on 'the country of your choice' – in our case, Guatemala. There are thirty questions. We can answer just one: 'What is the official religion of the country?' 'I know that – Roman Catholic,' I reply. We guess at a second – 'favourite sport' ... 'Football?' suggests Dom. Football is, after all, the most popular sport in the majority of countries, so it seems a safe bet. We fail to answer a single other question correctly ... oh dear, we have our homework cut out for us.

The importance of a good knowledge of the country, the culture and the people of Guatemala, so that we can bring our son up to know his background, is drummed into us during the course. It is essential we bring our son up to know his heritage. We are told this time and time again. Whilst Dom and I agree, at the same time we personally feel that too much emphasis is made over bringing the culture of our adopted child into our home. There must be a balance. Our son will be British as well as Guatemalan – Guatemalan by birth, British by upbringing – and we feel that it is important that he grows up feeling he belongs here. Too much emphasis on his past and his Guatemalan heritage, and he may feel an alien in the country he grows up in; too little explanation about his background and he will never feel comfortable in his country of birth if, one day, he chooses to return. We must get the balance right. We have a lot more research to do, and decide there and then that we will travel to Guatemala to discover more before we adopt a child from the country.

I fare a little better at the creative homework ... obviously I must be a child at heart. We are asked to prepare a picture for our future child to show him the link between his birth family and his adoptive family. I spend a happy Sunday afternoon drawing and cutting out shapes – a yellow octopus and a green octopus. I mount them on blue card (the sea) and entwine one leg of each octopus together. At this point I put a smiley face – our son – between the octopuses. The main body of each octopus – one the birth mummy and daddy, the other the adoptive mummy and daddy – is marked, and smiley faces on each leg indicate siblings, uncles, aunts and grandparents of both adoptive and birth families. It certainly appeals to the kid in me to spend all afternoon cutting out shapes and sticking them on paper, and I am ridiculously proud at the result. I am applauded by the group, who all want a copy. But more importantly, we hope it will earn a few more brownie points for us on our home-study report.

We watch a video of Romanian orphans left clinging to the bars of their cots, abandoned and rocking to and fro like caged, demented tigers at a zoo. It is a pathetic and heartbreaking sight and shows the damage that can be done to fragile children's brains if they are not given love and affection at an early stage. We learn how children who are left in an orphanage to be looked after by a number of carers but who never attach to one of them will become institutionalised at an early age, unable thereafter to properly bond or attach to even the most loving and caring adoptive parents. It is a truly heartbreaking sight and there is barely a dry eye in the room. It is also a sobering thought: even children as young as one year old are affected by their early experiences of institutionalised care.

We learn from our instructor about the impact of an adoption on the extended family – the child's birth family and the new adoptive family. We learn about heavy issues such as attachment disorder, separation and loss, child abuse – physical, emotional and sexual – foetal alcohol syndrome and the many other medical problems that one often has to expect with adopted children. As our instructor talks, we can see the realisation dawning on everyone's faces that there are a lot of uncertainties involved when you adopt a child.

We learn about the 'Sainsbury's moment' – that moment which happens all too frequently, apparently, in every intercountry adoptive parent's life. You are standing in the check-out queue at a super-market, when someone comments, 'Where is he from?' Fine. We can answer positively and without hesitation. But what about when they mutter as an aside to someone else, 'Mmm ... more immigrants. She should have taken one from her own country, don't you think?' Harder to deal with. Or, worse still, when they directly address your child with, 'So, where is your *real* mummy and daddy then?' It seems unbelievable that people say these things, but apparently they do. We must be prepared.

We are divided into smaller groups for various role-play sessions in which we have to act something out and report back to the group at large. One of the scenarios we have to enact is making the decision on how and what to tell your adoptive child about their background if you know they are the result of a rape. Scenarios like this are emotionally draining and frankly terrifying, but they are a useful lesson and insight into the possible problems ahead. Adoption is not an easy option, we see, and the route we are taking will not be an easy one. What we are about to do is not something to be taken lightly, but what we are learning does not diminish our intentions. We are just as determined as ever to adopt a child and become a family.

We all feel that the course concentrates so much on the potential problems that it gives little reminder of the joys that will also be experienced. In spite of that, Dom and I consider that it is an excellent course, though I can certainly see why many PAPs are put off pursuing further the route of adoption. (Of the ten couples and one single adopter starting out on the course, more than half decide, for one reason or another, not to continue with the adoption process.)

We make good friends on the course – other couples who are at a similar stage and who have similar, goals, experiences, hopes and fears. It really does help to be able to discuss what we are going through with others at a similar stage, and we expect to remain friends with some of them in the future.

One couple describe this preparation course as their moment of conception, the moment their future child is conceived. This is indeed where the journey truly begins – though we know we still have a long way to go.

Unexpectedly, at this point it is the prospect of becoming a parent that I am finding more frightening than the prospect of the problems the child may or may not have as a result of being adopted. It is during this course that I really wonder for the first time how I will actually cope with a baby. I am concerned that I know so little about babies – I have reached the not-so-tender age of forty four, without so much as ever having changed a nappy! How will I cope when a baby suddenly arrives without the preparation of anti-natal classes that women attend who are having their own birth child? I leave one session in tears of concern at this prospect. Dom is wonderful; he is so supportive, so caring, so understanding. He comforts me, reminds me we have family close by for support, and that every soon-to-be mother must experience these fears at some stage. I will be all right.

The preparation course is excellent, but we are struggling to find the support and information required to further our own case, to research our chosen country from where we will adopt and to find out the ins and outs of the process. There seems to be a negative attitude by many in this country towards ICA, and certainly our government ministers and the Department for Children, Schools and Families has done nothing to encourage such adoptions or improve their standing. In other European countries and in the United States, ICA is positively encouraged. Here, the opposite is true. The lack of official support; lack of government backing and lack of information provided must surely be the main contributory factors as to why Britain has one of the lowest rates of ICA in the developed world.

Spain processes 8,000 ICA applications a year, the United States and France over 4,000 each, but Britain deals with fewer than 400 applications a year. Even Norway, with a population one twelfth of our population, receives almost twice as many adopted children a year as we do, and Ireland, with a population one fifteenth that of the UK, receives more children than the UK does.

The adoption process in Britain is to blame and is very off-putting in so many ways – first, in the number of countries available. In principle there are hundreds of countries to choose from, but in reality there are only a few that you can deal with via their governments or through agencies, many of whom are based in the United States. If you wish to adopt from the rest – many other countries – you are fighting the legal system of a far-off country, often in a language different from your own – no wonder it is off-putting. Not to mention the fact that each country has its own list of requirements and restrictions regarding age, religion, number of years married, and so on, which mean that you may not be eligible for consideration in the first place.

Then there is the home-study course that you have to complete in England, regardless of whether you are adopting domestically or intercountry. If you are adopting intercountry it will be designed for the specific country you have chosen. The process itself involves much bureaucracy, can take months, or even years, and can involve massive costs and problems with the Home Office and the government of the country you are adopting from. If, for whatever reason, that country closes its doors to adoption when you are midway through the process or the whole case falls through due to some technicality, you are left high and dry, having incurred massive costs proving your 'interest' in the country in order that you may be taken seriously enough to pass the panel. You may have done a course to learn the language, visited the country, and so on. Apart from the emotional upheaval, all this adds up financially, and it is not easy to suddenly switch to another country. Many such horror stories happen largely because the process reflects the politics between countries rather than the humanitarian aspect of adopting a needy child, which is really what it should be about. The process is meant to work for the benefit of the children, yet so often in reality this is not the case.

The costs involved when you adopt from overseas are substantial. If you adopt domestically, the government pays all the costs of the process. If you adopt from overseas then you need to cover the costs yourself and, depending on the country from which you are adopting, you are talking about anything between £15,000 and £40,000 when you figure in everything, including the various travel trips you will need to take. Not everyone has sufficient funds or can raise this kind of cash. It is a tragic reality that many couples who wish to adopt and who would make ideal loving parents are turned away by the restrictive English system and are unable to afford intercountry adoption.

Last but by no means least, the public perception of ICA is very negative in Britain. Reports – many grossly over-exaggerated – of child trafficking, together with the speed with which certain celebrity adoptions appear to have taken place, have not helped matters. The belief that children should remain in their country of origin is held by many in this country, and indeed I too believe that where possible this is the best option for a child. In a perfect world there would be no place for ICA. However, where it is not possible for a child to be cared for within its own birth family, extended family or community, and where there is little or no social welfare programme to provide for a child, ICA must be considered as a viable and favourable option. Certainly intercountry adoption is a better alternative for a child than growing up in an orphanage or on the streets and as such it should be encouraged, as long as the new adoptive family can offer the secure and loving family that every child deserves, and on the understanding that they will encourage their child's knowledge of his or her culture and heritage.

Intercountry adoption is certainly not for the faint-hearted.

7

Everything ...
Including Your Inside Leg Measurement

October – December 2006

The dreaded home-study course: long months of probing assessment.

We are on tenterhooks all the time, for every minute of every session with our social worker. Alisha could not be a kinder, more sympathetic person, but all the same, we know we are being judged, every word noted, every expression analysed. Any sign of weakness queried. We are giving truthful answers to her every question, but at the same time we are terrified of giving the wrong impression.

Alisha is writing down every word we say, every emotion we convey, every impression she gets. Everything will be written in her report: the home study. We understand this can be sixty to eighty pages long. An independent social worker will read it and then return to interview us with any further questions she feels the report raises. The report will then be sent to our panel judges to read prior to our assessment at panel. Panel ... the moment of truth; the moment when we will hopefully be confirmed as eligible to adopt a baby from Guatemala.

We have done a lot more research on Guatemala, on the process of adoption from that country, on its history and culture, and on adoption in general. We have read a number of books; attended a day-long lecture on the health and development of internationally adopted children and even started to learn Spanish at an evening adult education course. We are preparing ourselves in every way we think we can for the home study and for adopting a child from Guatemala.

We are asked about any significant previous relationships. We spend one entire three-hour session talking about my previous marriage – why I got married, what my relationship was like with my ex-husband; what went wrong; I am even asked about our sex life ... is this really relevant? My ex-husband is contacted, questioned about our relationship and whether he thinks I would make a good parent. I am lucky that we are still on reasonably good terms. He gives me a glowing report, saying he could not think of anyone better suited to being a good mum. Thank you 'Ex'. I am truly grateful.

We are questioned about our childhood and our parents' parenting techniques; our relationships with our parents, siblings and friends; our schooling; our jobs and hobbies; our likes and our dislikes.

It is intrusive; painfully so. Much of the questioning is entirely justified – after all, the welfare of a child is at stake – but a lot of it seems to go way beyond what we would consider was a necessary and justified amount of investigation. Hour after hour after hour of intensive questioning ... we feel we are being interrogated.

Any issue which caused a problem in our lives is analysed in minute detail and we are asked to write about it. I have to write about my father's alcoholism, the effect it had on my childhood and the effect it has on me now. Dom has to write about being bullied at school. We find it painful to have to go over these details. I feel disloyal having to discuss my father and his problems with a stranger. It is hard not to just turn round and say, 'None of your business.' Alisha tries to make it easier for us; she is just doing her job, but honestly, is so much detail really necessary?

One of the hardest sessions we have is the one discussing my miscarriage and our attempts for me to become pregnant again. We had been warned that our social worker would think it important to ensure that we had come to terms with my infertility if we were considering adopting, and indeed we agreed this was important. I think I have – we have – come to terms with it as much as we ever will, but it doesn't make it any easier to discuss the saddest and hardest experience that either of us have ever had to face; it is not easy to be asked question after question about how we felt then; how we feel now. I even have to write a piece about it for Alisha.

We are asked for assurances that we are taking preventative measures now to ensure I will not become pregnant. This is a policy most local authorities are quite strict about for couples considering adoption. It seems crazy after all this time trying to get pregnant to have to actively prevent it. Initially we feel at odds with this pressure to avoid pregnancy, but as the months go by and we see what is involved with adopting a child, we can see the value of this advice.

I have to write an essay about what Catholicism means to me. We had already discussed religion at length and Alisha is aware that we have decided any children we have will be brought up as Catholics. Although Dom is not a Catholic, he is happy about this, feeling that a good grounding in religion is important and that as I am the one regularly attending church services, it makes sense for our son to be brought up in the same religion as myself. Our social worker seems dubious. We are questioned again and again on the subject – does she think I am some kind of weird religious fanatic? I mean, it is not as if I am saying I worship Satan or belong to some strange sect. Catholicism is pretty mainstream, I would have thought.

We do have a lighter moment when we discuss the various religions in Guatemala. When we first considered Guatemala as a country from which to adopt, one of the attractions to me, as a practising Catholic, was that it is a Catholic country and that we will therefore be bringing up our son practising the same religion he would have done had he remained in his native country. I commented on how we were comfortable with this situation, but how we had noticed that a large number of those in the Maya communities still worshipped their pagan gods as well as 'officially' being Catholic. With a perfectly straight face and not a trace of irony, Alisha asked if we would also be bringing up José to worship the pagan gods as well. I knew I could not answer – I suddenly had an uncontrollable urge to giggle – I had this wonderful vision of a large statue of Maximón – one of Guatemala's most popular gods who is dressed like a bandit and smokes a cigar – sitting perched in the corner of our kitchen with offerings of alcohol and flowers placed in front of him, as is the Guatemalan practice. The thought was just too ridiculous for words. What would it be – a crucifix in one corner, Maximón in another? Fortunately, Dom – kicked by me under the table to answer – comes to my rescue. 'Well you see,' he says, with a perfectly straight face, 'much as we would love to find out which particular pagan god they worship in the village our son will come from, it would be so terrible if we got it wrong. Probably best just to stick to Catholicism, I think.' I cough to cover my giggles. Thank you Dom.

Alisha is kind, sensitive and very sweet. Two flowerpots high, with a mane of beautiful long black curly hair and a gentle manner, she makes every effort to try and ensure we feel at ease. We had heard such horror stories of social workers being prejudiced against you from the start, particularly if you are middle class, just waiting for a moment to catch you out and prove that you would not be fit to be adoptive parents. We heard of one family being asked to change their surname so that a child might be able to say it more easily; of another family being told that their middle-class lifestyle would prevent them from adopting as their social worker believed that it meant that they would have too little in common with the background of the children needing adopting; and of another family failing panel due to the judges feeling their intellectual status was too high (both had masters degrees) and believing that they would therefore expect too much of any child adopted who perhaps had an inferior intelligence level. We have no such experiences with our social worker. We are lucky – Alisha appears to be on our side, right from the start.

All the same, it is not easy getting used to the incessant, probing questions. As one adoptive parent warned us, 'Your social worker will want to know everything about you, and *I mean everything* – inside leg measurement, the lot.' Boy, was she right. It is not a comfortable feeling baring one's soul to a complete stranger, particularly a stranger who holds your future, your deepest desire, in the palm of her hand. If her report is favourable, the panel are likely to approve us as adoptive parents; if it is not favourable … well, we are unlikely even to be put before them. Is it right that one person – one social worker – should have so much power?

We also have to get used to the 'touchy feely' response to our replies. It is a different way of communicating from that which we are used to. We British, with our stiff upper lips, are not used to answering the queries along the lines of 'How did it make you feel?' and 'Do you feel you have come to terms with this?' that are given by her to every life experience we relate. We get by … at least we hope we have.

Then there is the paperwork. One woman wrote, in an article I read on the adoption process, that the best way to explain the home-study paperwork is to think of every form you have ever filled in during your lifetime and then multiply that by one hundred. This would give you some idea of what is involved. She was not exaggerating. I calculate that we have spent approximately forty-five hours filling in the sixteen forms, essays and profiles that we have so far been asked to complete for our adoption application, and we still have a long way to go and many more forms to complete before we can finally bring our son home.

21 December 2006

Finally, after nine sessions, each lasting three hours, Alisha has completed her questioning. It now remains for her to meet our referees – one family member (one of my sisters) and a long-standing friend of each of us – and then write her home-study report to be sent to our panel judges. Even our family and friends have to do their homework for us – our referees are sent long questionnaires in advance which they have to fill in and return. We are grateful.

It is infuriating that although our home-study meetings were completed today, we will now have to wait until the end of March – three whole months – before we go to panel and can progress any further. The reason? Alisha, our social worker, is taking extended leave and going on holiday to her homeland – India – and we apparently cannot go to panel without her. Therefore we have to wait. As if the process is not long enough in the first place. It is just our luck that she should take a sabbatical now. Whilst we are pleased to have had such an understanding social worker, we cannot help wondering whether our local authority should not have foreseen this delay and perhaps assigned us someone who could see our case through to panel without such an unnecessary delay. Very annoying indeed.

26 January 2007

I have just read a BBC press report, 'Babies Removed to Meet Targets', by political reporter Brian Wheeler, stating that babies are being removed from their parents in England and Wales so that councils can meet adoption targets. MPs are concerned that the rise in the number of young children being taken into care is linked to pressure on councils to increase adoption rates. In 2000, ministers set a target of a 50 per cent increase by March 2006 in the number of children in local authority care being adopted, and according to the latest available figures, the number of 'looked after' children being adopted rose by 37.7 per cent between 2000 and 2004. Liberal Democrat MP John Hemming has evidence from people who had contacted him to complain that children are being separated from their parents without proper grounds. He says that a thousand children a year are being removed from their birth parents just to satisfy targets. 'A national scandal.'

This is not the first report of this nature that I have recently seen and it turns my blood cold. Is this *really* the case? BAAF denies that this is happening, but who do you believe? Can you imagine finding out that you have innocently adopted a child that had been removed from his or her birth family without true justification? It does not bear thinking about. The powers that the local authorities seem to possess are terrifying, and not for the first time, we feel grateful that we have made the decision to adopt from overseas.

2 March 2007

We have received a copy of our home-study report (known as Form F) from Alisha: a copy of the lengthy report which will be submitted to the panel judges. It is a great report; very thorough, very positive, and even glowing in parts. It is with much relief that we read the final paragraph, which states that, in conclusion, she recommends that the panel approve us as a suitable couple to adopt a child from Guatemala. Thank you, Alisha. Let us hope the panel judges agree.

8

Our First Taste of Guatemala

March 2007

What better way to spend the time between the finish of our home-study sessions and our panel date than with a visit to Guatemala, the country from where we hope to adopt our son?

It is important to us that we learn as much as we can about the place that will be our son's country of origin. We have been reading a lot about Guatemala over the last few months, but really feel a need to experience it first hand. We are aware that when we go there on our visit trip (to meet our son for the first time) and on the pick-up trip (to take him home), we will be based in Guatemala City, with little opportunity of seeing the rest of the country, so we have decided to take a week's holiday – all we can manage with our busy work schedules at the moment – and attempt to see as much as we can of the country of Guatemala.

18 March 2007

What an experience. We have just returned from a truly amazing holiday in Guatemala. We packed in as many places and as many experiences as we could in one week, trying to see as much of the country and to experience as much of the culture as was possible. Dom and I are both quite widely travelled – we both organise corporate events and conferences all over the world – but we feel that we have seen few places as beautiful as Guatemala.

Guatemala is a stunning country with an incredible variety of landscapes – from volcanoes to lakes, jungles to beaches, colonial towns to tiny villages – and has such beautiful, friendly people with their warm, open smiles, black hair, golden coffee-brown skin and large, dark brown, almond-shaped eyes; and as for the children – well, I could happily have taken home any number of the angelic-looking little tots we came across.

Guatemala is an immensely colourful country, with the traditional costumes the Maya people wear and the fabrics they weave; the markets; the cemeteries in which they bury their dead; the birds and the flowers; and the houses in Antigua. There are gloriously vibrant colours wherever one looks.

Known as 'the land of eternal spring', Guatemala has a near-perfect climate. It is warm and sunny throughout the year, and on the whole not too blisteringly hot or humid, except in the northern lowlands (the jungle region), where it is very hot and sticky.

The following are just some of our experiences.

8–10 March 2007

Noisy, dirty, smelly ... the smell of the exhaust fumes from the so-called Chicken Buses (ancient American school buses shipped over to Guatemala, and the only means of public transportation round the country); the noise of the traffic, and in particular the noise of these buses; the smog. This is our first experience of Guatemala City, the capital city of Guatemala.

Fortunately, our brief first experience of Guatemala City is certainly not representative of the rest of the country. Immediately on landing, we take a taxi through only a small part of the city en route to Antigua, the old colonial capital, some forty-five minutes drive away, where we will spend the first two days of our holiday.

What a contrast! Driving into Antigua is like entering a film set. We had seen photographs of the picturesque cobbled streets and brightly coloured houses, but imagined this to be one street only, or one small area, widely photographed for the tourist brochures. Not a bit of it. Every street we enter is similarly decorative.

Antigua is the former colonial capital of Guatemala and one of the Americas' most enchanting colonial cities. It was founded as Santiago (which means St James) in 1543 after a mudslide destroyed the previous capital, Ciudad Vieja, located a few kilometres away on the flanks of a volcano, the Volcán de Agua.

At its peak, Antigua was apparently the third most important city in the Spanish Empire, after Mexico City and Lima. It had thirty-eight churches, a cathedral and a thriving community, but in the eighteenth century it was repeatedly destroyed by earthquakes and rebuilt, until finally, in 1776, after a great earthquake destroyed the city once more, the capital was transferred to Guatemala City and Antigua was evacuated. From 1830, it began to grow once more and became known as La Antigua Guatemala, which means Old Guatemala. During the civil war (1960–1996), Antiguans hid at home and visitors were rare, but once peace was restored, Antigua was transformed and visitors returned. Antigua is now a UNESCO World Heritage Site.

Walking through the cobbled streets of this stunning colonial town, past the brightly coloured buildings, we couldn't help but notice the beautiful interiors and courtyards of many of the beautifully preserved – or restored – old colonial houses. Many of the buildings are baroque in style, some are Moorish, and others look more Venetian, with wrought-iron 'Juliet' balconies. Almost all of them open onto picturesque courtyards, just glimpsed from the streets, with carved arches and pretty little fountains, and filled with exotic purple, orange, pink and white flowers – bougainvillea, jasmine and hibiscus. The sight of these little courtyards, the smell of the flowers and the trickling sound of the fountains is a charming sensory experience.

The Maya people seem warm and friendly, and are very smiley. Many of the women, in particular, are as brightly dressed as the houses. We were surprised to see so many in the traditional hand-loomed costumes, but apparently, so proud are they of their heritage in the hillside villages, that most of them still wear these outfits. You can tell where they are from by their *huipiles* (traditional blouses). In one village these will be patterned with blue and purple zigzags; in another, red and black stripes, in a third, embroidered birds, and so on. In addition, the style in which they dress their long black hair varies from village to village. For example, in Santiago, the women wrap a 60-foot length of fabric round their head into a sort of headband resembling a hat brim, to mimic the halo around a full moon during the rainy season.

The inhabitants of Antigua are known as *panza verde*, which means 'green belly', on account of the large number of avocados they eat. In fact, in Guatemala there are so many different types of avocado, all ripening at various times of the year, that on every single day of the calendar you can find a ripe avocado. Bliss.

Arriving on Thursday night, we spent Friday and Saturday exploring Antigua. We hired a guide to explain the history of the city, and our tour included an interesting visit to some of the churches partially destroyed by earthquakes. Their remains have been restored and they still operate as churches.

On Saturday our pre-planned visit to an orphanage – a *hogar*, as they are called in Guatemala – was both the high point and the low point of the trip. It was clean; the babies were well looked after and the staff were wonderful – friendly and caring – but you could not get away from the fact that here you had so many babies abandoned and relinquished; and that they are in an institution. The staff simply do not have the time or the manpower to give the babies the attention they crave and need – the interaction that is so important at this stage of their development. Like many orphanages the world over, they do not have the funds to provide the extra staff for this role. The babies are washed; they are fed; they are changed; and they are popped back in their cots. End of story.

Fifty-two little bundles in rows of cots; it was heartbreaking. The temptation to just grab one and run was immense, but even if one were foolish enough to do so, how would a choice be made? I realised, for the first time, that we were lucky that the choice would be made for us. How on earth could anyone make that decision?

Choosing one baby over another would be beyond me. I wanted them all. 'I don't think we really have the room for fifty-two babies,' Dom said gently, as he led me from the room. I managed to stem my tears until we arrived back at our hotel, where I broke down and sobbed for these little ones. It is just so heartbreaking that there are so many children whose birth mothers are, for whatever reasons, unable to keep them. What must go through the minds of these women during pregnancy? Whilst they are giving birth? How can they bear to give up these little angels? What agonies must they go through in giving up these children? Those poor women; these poor babies.

If ever there had been any doubt over whether we were doing the right thing, our visit to the *hogar* would have eliminated it. Not that we had any doubt, but intercountry adoption does not always get a good press and it is hard to be immune to all the criticisms. Not now though – after this visit we became even more determined than ever that we could make a difference to one little life. A child should be brought up in their own country; their own culture, but – and it is a big but – if that country and that culture cannot give the child a family and a good future, then surely it is better that he or she should be with a family who can provide for him or her and give the child a future. We will love a child and will give him a future. We are doing the right thing.

11 March 2007

The following day, Sunday, we hired a car and driver to take us to the little town of Chichicastenango – what a great name, but trying saying that after a few glasses of wine! Located in the highlands of Guatemala, Chichicastenango is famous for its twice-weekly markets, but we had also been told that it is a good example of a highland town, and that the journey would take us through some typical highland scenery.

The country of Guatemala is largely made up of the lowlands or rainforest region in the north, and the highlands, which cover much of the rest of the country with rugged and dramatic scenery of mountains, mountain lakes and a great chain of volcanoes which run from Antigua to the Mexican border. The highlands are home to a high percentage of Guatemala's indigenous Maya (or Mayan) people. Their villages are scattered amongst the mountains, many of them very remote, and plenty still without vehicle access. The Maya communities are to a large extent cut off from the rest of the country; they maintain their traditional customs, rites, religions and costumes dating back hundreds, sometimes thousands, of years, and between them speak twenty-two Maya dialects rather than the 'national' language of Spanish. To a large extent the Maya way of life remains remarkably untouched by modernity.

During the thirty-six-year civil war, which commenced in 1960 and which was fought between leftist guerrillas and the government, the highlands were targeted heavily by both guerrillas and the army. Merciless death squads killed thousands of Maya people, and hundreds of their villages were razed to the ground in the military's scorched-earth campaigns, in the hope of choking off civilian support for guerrillas. It is estimated that 200,000 people were killed, 40,000 went missing and thousands fled over the border into Mexico. The missing were victims of the 'forced disappearance' state-sponsored abductions in which the victim was never seen again nor accounted for. The civil war ended in 1996 and the people living in many of the highland villages are still struggling to recover to this day.

After a tortuous ascent up into the mountains, along a seemingly endless series of switchback roads, we reached the isolated town of Chichicastenango.

A Quiché Maya town located 2,030 metres above the valley floor, Chichicastenango was founded in 1550 by Dominican missionaries, but has since become more of a centre for those with pre-Christian beliefs who congregate on Sundays to hold their ceremonies outside, and rather more bizarrely inside, the otherwise Catholic church. I must admit to rather an uncomfortable feeling on entering the Catholic church in the centre of town and hearing the chanting to the pagan gods, as the Maya people covered large areas of the floor of the church with flowers and broken stubs of candles. I understand that the Catholic priests tolerate these pagan forms of worship in their churches, but to someone used to a more traditional use of a Catholic church, these rituals and the sight of statues of saints dressed in gaudy Mayan robes did seem quite extraordinary. I found myself quite unable to pray and felt almost blasphemous being in a Catholic church surrounded by people worshipping pagan gods.

As is the Maya custom, the worshippers had lit a fire by the entrance to the church and were burning their offerings before entering the building. The steps to the church were almost blocked with people performing this ritual of worship. Perforated cans in which incense was being burnt were laid on the steps amongst candles and flowers, and the soft hum of murmured prayers filled the air, almost drowned out by a louder chanting played through a sound system outside the church.

In addition to the religious ceremonies, many local residents and countless tourists also flock to Chichicastenango for its twice-weekly market. There has been a market here for hundreds, if not thousands, of years and every Thursday and Sunday, the streets are lined with stalls on which sellers display their merchandise. The inhabitants of the various Maya communities in the mountains surrounding the town descend early with their wares. Many walk for hours to get there, some even leaving the night before and bedding down at the roadside to be there early and get a good pitch; others travel by truck, crammed in and hanging off the back in a manner which would certainly give our health and safety inspectors in the UK a seizure. At dawn the vendors lay out their wares – brightly coloured fabrics authentically woven, colourful wooden masks, pottery, belts, clothes, flowers, fruit and vegetables. It creates a kaleidoscope of colour, from the vivid red of the piles of chillies and tomatoes, to the green of the baskets of avocados, the piles of yellow corn and bananas, and the rows of brightly coloured flowers; even the vendors themselves contribute to the rich array of colours in their brightly embroidered *huipiles*.

The choice was overwhelming; from textiles and handicrafts for tourists, to everyday items for the villagers (clothing, toys, soap, fruit and vegetables), and you can find just about everything somewhere in the market. It is impossible not to get lost, but doing so is all part of the fun.

The market was a total sensory overload – a bright, colourful, noisy, exhausting crush, and an experience not to be missed. We were worn out by the time we left, laden with haggled-over souvenirs and birthday and Christmas presents for our family and friends back home.

12 March 2007

With the shrill twittering of birds at dawn, the waters of the lake calmly lapping the shore, and the surrounding volcanoes rising into the early-morning mist, encircling Lake Atitlan, this perfectly peaceful haven to which we had travelled the night before was in stark contrast to the bustling market at Chichicastenango.

Lake Atitlan (Lago de Atitlán) is considered by many to be the most beautiful lake in the world, and we could easily see why. As Aldous Huxley aptly said in 1934, in his travel book *Beyond the Mexique Bay*, 'Lake Como, it seems to me, touches the limit of the permissibly picturesque; but Atitlan is Como with the additional embellishments of several immense volcanoes. It is really too much of a good thing. After a few days of this impossible landscape one finds oneself thinking nostalgically of the English Home Counties.'

Lake Atitlan is, indeed, astonishingly beautiful. Formed 80,000 years ago by a violent volcanic eruption, it is the deepest lake in Central America and is encircled by volcanoes and steep hills. The surrounding villages have been home to many different Maya communities since 1000 BC and earlier, and the Maya culture is still as strong in most of the inhabitants today. They continue to wear the traditional Maya costumes and follow the old Maya customs, rites and ways of life.

The surface of the lake is normally calm and clear in the mornings, but by early afternoon the *xocomil* ('the wind that carries away sin') blows in from the coast, churning the surface and making travel by boat quite a rocky experience, as we were to find out later that day when we crossed the lake by boat to go horse riding around the base and up the flanks of one of the volcanoes.

The scenery surrounding the lake just cries out to be explored, but we had been warned that foreigners walking along isolated paths are an all-too-easy target for bandits and unfortunately it is unsafe to explore the mountains without a guide. We had therefore decided that instead we would discover something of the highlands on horseback, with a guide. Horse riding is a great way of exploring the real hinterland of a country, areas that are inaccessible to vehicles, and one can cover a greater distance on horseback than on foot, particularly when limited by time. Dom and I have explored some of the terrain of quite a few countries in this way.

As it turned out, we were right to have been cautious and go with a guide. Our little group of four tourists – Dom and I, and a couple from America – were escorted by two armed guides on horseback and a pack (I exaggerate not!) of rather vicious-looking dogs. The owners of the stables had suggested we lock any money and other valuables in their safe at the stables. We spent a very enjoyable few hours trekking through the coffee and macadamia nut plantations, and up the flanks of one of the volcanoes to a col from where, on a clear day (today, sadly, was not sufficiently clear), one can apparently see all the way to the Pacific Ocean. On our return trek, as our path crossed a little road winding its way up the volcano, we were overtaken by a jeep in which sat four or five locals. They screeched to a halt and sat in the middle of the road in our way, staring at us in an uncomfortably threatening manner but saying nothing. Our guide very calmly and slowly dismounted and indicated to us to remain mounted but to slowly follow behind him. He walked, head down, avoiding eye contact and neither looking to the right nor the left, straight past the jeep. He was obviously showing them respect: 'We want no trouble; just let us on our way.' You could feel the tension in the air, but the moment passed without incident. It did, however, serve as an indication to us of the caution one has to take in the more isolated parts of this country.

13 March 2007

Today we spent an incredible day experiencing a little of the day-to-day existence of the Maya communities in the highlands of Guatemala.

Guatemala has a small, rich ladino ruling class and a large (mainly Maya) exploited working class. Little has been done to improve the lot of this indigenous population, the Maya Indians, since the end of the 36-year civil war. Less than 1 per cent of export-orientated agricultural producers still control 75 per cent of the best land and the indigenous people are still left to survive through seeking labour via seasonal migration, or from what they can grow (corn, avocados and other fruit and vegetables) on the tiny patches of land, called *milpas*, where they live. All the work is done by hand. There are no mechanical instruments; no tractors, no donkeys, no horses, no oxen. They take the surplus yield to market to sell for other items essential for their existence, but life is incredibly hard.

We were fortunate to have a Maya guide, as this meant we could go off the beaten track to visit communities tourists do not usually get to see, and even go into people's homes. First we visited the Maya town of Solola, overlooking Lake Atitlan. We wandered through the busy, crowded fruit and vegetable market and went to a local cemetery, which was quite an extraordinary experience. The afterlife is very important to the Maya people, and the Maya cemeteries are immensely colourful. Those who can afford it are buried in brightly painted tombs, above ground, and the engravings on the tomb stone are of images representing the lives they led – for example, a book for a teacher or a plough or other farm implement for a farmer. Family members are buried in boxes laid one on top of the other within the tomb, and once the family boxes reach five layers, the tombs are razed to the ground and the family members start the tomb all over again on the same plot. Those who cannot afford elaborate tombs, and there are many – the majority, in fact – are buried in a box in a row that resembles a unit of shelves. The row of boxes reaches the whole length of the graveyard – perhaps forty boxes in length and five rows (boxes) high. A handwritten note on the foot of the box gives the name and date of death of the occupant.

Every aspect of Maya life, from the birth of a child to the planting of corn, is full of religious significance, and today the Maya life is a complicated fusion of Maya and Catholic religions. Christ and the saints have taken their place alongside their pagan gods of the heavens and lords of the underworld. As our Maya guide described herself, in common with most Maya people, she is 'Catholic on the outside, Maya on the inside'. Outwardly the Maya practise the Catholic religion of the country, but in reality most of them worship their own pagan gods: the first corn god, the second corn god, and so on. They have a very strong belief in the underworld, which they say the Catholics do not yet understand. Outward rituals of Catholicism are used to worship the ancient forms, a compromise which was agreed by the Spanish priests trying to convert the country to Christianity. Many of our Christian saints are worshipped by the Maya, but these saints also represent their pagan gods. For example, Maximón, a drinking, smoking ladino figure, is the Fifth Lord of the Underworld, but is also called San Simon or sometimes referred to as Judas. He is perhaps the most surreal manifestation of the hybrid ancient Mayan-Catholic belief system of the Maya people.

A statue of Maximón lives in the home of one of the villagers, and every year or so he is moved, in a big ceremony, to another home, the occupants of whom will host his stay. It is a great honour to have Maximón stay with you. We were lucky enough to be able to visit the home in which he was currently residing in a tiny highland village called Concepcion. It was a simple home, but one room had been set aside for this most prestigious of visitors. The room was decked out with a rather weird combination of Christian and Mayan images. In the centre was an altar on which there were statues of

Christian saints and a large crucifix, as well as a skull and crossbones and various Maya images as well. To one side of the altar, seated on a chair, was a life-size image of Maximón, a ladino gentleman with a large moustache, dressed like a bandit and smoking a cigar. The local people bring him offerings of alcohol and flowers, and he is a vital and important part of their religion and daily life of worship.

The Maya cross was displayed in this room, as it was on most of the tombs we saw in the cemetery. It is similar to the Christian crucifix except that the arms are the same length as the upright part of the cross. It is used to signify the four winds of heaven, the four directions (north, south, east and west), and everlasting life.

The poverty of these villages was so striking. Many of the homes were barely more than a few planks of wood with a piece of corrugated iron for a roof. There is often no running water, no electricity. In one of the homes we visited, girls as young as nine or ten were sitting on the ground sorting a huge pile of corn; in another, a couple of children no more than six or seven years old were left to fend for themselves whilst their father tended the corn in the fields and their mother visited the market.

Not for the first time we wondered whether our little 'José' would come from a home like this. Quite probably.

In one of the larger homes we visited, a room had been set aside for worship of the Maya gods and it had been filled with ancient Maya artefacts found in the fields the occupants tilled. These artefacts – carved stones which could be hundreds, or maybe even thousands, of years old – should probably be in a museum, but to the Maya who dug them up, they are simply the symbols of worship of their ancestors and as such will continue to be used for worship in their homes.

In each house we were welcomed by smiling faces, friendly nods and inquisitive stares. We were concerned not to be seen as intruding – the last thing we wanted was to insult these proud people in any way by our presence – but our guide explained that she personally knew all the families we were visiting and told us that they felt honoured to have guests from such a far-off land. We gave them a small amount of money as we left, in gratitude for their hospitality, and their grateful smiles and nods showed just how very welcome a little extra money was to them. This had been the perfect intro-duction to the real Guatemala, and we felt not only honoured that these people had welcomed us into their homes, but also quite humbled by the experience.

Later that night, we flew from Guatemala City to the island-city of Flores, in the El Petén region of northern Guatemala, in order to visit the ancient Maya site of Tikal.

14 March 2007

In the lowlands of northern Guatemala, bordering the country of Belize, the El Petén region is covered in thick jungle and is very sparsely populated. The few visitors the region sees come purely to visit Tikal, one of the most famous ancient Maya sites ever discovered.

Tikal means 'Place of the Voices', and it was built between 900 BC and AD 900. It is possibly the most magnificent of all Maya sites and consists of more than ten thousand buildings and temples, of which only four thousand so far have been recovered from this part of the jungle; a site of 576 square kilometres which is now a protected national park.

By the time of Christ, around two thousand years ago, Tikal was already established as an important site with a large permanent population. A ruling dynasty was established and the great warrior leaders turned Tikal into the most elaborate and magnificent of all Maya city-states. Mayan art and architecture developed, becoming increasingly ornate, and magnificent soaring temples were built for the leaders and to honour their gods. By the beginning of the ninth century AD, severe signs of crisis emerged across the entire Maya region, possibly as a result of a period of drought, and the popu-lation of Tikal declined. No one knows the reason for the final downfall of Tikal, but by the tenth century AD the site had been effectively abandoned.

Tikal lay largely forgotten and overgrown by the dense rainforest for several centuries until a chance discovery by a Spanish padre, Father Avandano, in 1695. Lost in the swamps of El Petén, he stumbled across some 'old buildings', but the colonial powers were unimpressed. In 1848 a government expedition rediscovered the site. This was followed by expeditions by the Swiss scientist Dr Gustav Bernoulli and the English archaeologist Alfred Maudslay, but it was 1956 before a project – led by the American archaeologist William R. Coe – was started to disinter Tikal from the almost impenetrable jungle and restore this great Mayan city.

Many of the buildings and temples still lie undiscovered under the tropical vegetation of the jungle, inhabited by jaguars, spider monkeys, howler monkeys, crocodiles, many different snakes and spiders and a great number of brightly coloured birds.

We set off at 4 a.m. to walk with our guide in the pitch dark into the heart of the jungle towards the site of Tikal, so that we could climb one of the temples before dawn. The trek was longer than I had expected and I found it quite a nerve-racking experience. We walked fast in order to get there before dawn broke, and were told to remain alert for snakes and spiders – a little difficult when we only had the small beams from a couple of torches with which to view our surroundings. I have always had a complete phobia about snakes, and as I imagined every raised root across which we stepped to be a snake, my heart was in my mouth. It was certainly with some relief that we climbed the final rungs of a rickety and very slippery wooden stepladder up out of the jungle onto a temple from whose dizzy height we could safely survey the world of the rainforest below.

Sitting atop Temple IV, which rises two hundred and twelve feet above the rainforest, and watching dawn break over the jungle was the most magical and awe-inspiring experience of my life. As soon as first light appeared, the jungle broke into a cacophony of sound, a symphony of screeches, hoots and other tropical noises, as howler monkeys and birds competed to make the greatest din. The sound was all around us and it was truly spine-tingling. Much of the jungle was shrouded in a mist which hangs over the canopy of trees each day until burnt off by the sun later in the morning, but peeping up through the mist one could just make out the pyramid shape of other temples rising above the rich and deep verdant blanket of trees, the never-ending green of the jungle. A toucan flew by at eye level and lanky spider monkeys swung through the trees below us, as the sun begun to show itself above the forest canopy.

As quickly as it started, the chorus faded. It was an extraordinary sound and a scene no camera can do justice to, but one we will remember for ever.

We saw a great many monkeys that morning, a vast array of brilliantly coloured birds, and even a crocodile. We heard a jaguar go by – well, that could have been an exaggeration by the guide for the benefit of us tourists, who knows – certainly there are jaguars living in this part of the jungle – but we did not catch a glimpse of this most beautiful of wild cats. We saw a giant tarantula but, to my immense relief, we saw no snakes. Guatemala has more varieties of snakes than any other country in the world, and our guide was anticipating pointing out many of the varieties. He exclaimed that it was a disappointing and unusual morning not to have seen any. Somehow I could not quite share his disappointment.

Dom and I returned to our hotel at lunchtime, and spent an afternoon relaxing by Lake Petén Itzá. Having been assured that the crocodiles were on the other side of the lake and never ventured over this side, we swam in the lake – though I did leave the water rather hurriedly when a log floated by – and we even took a little trip in a couple of canoes we found by the lake. It was idyllic.

15 March 2007

Guatemala City is dirty, crowded, polluted and with little architectural merit. Levels of poverty and crime are high and drug gangs rule the roost. The rubbish tip on the edge of the city is home to thousands of people who live a desperate and dangerous life sorting through the garbage for food and any item they may be able to sell.

Thousands of children who have been abandoned or who have run away from desperate situations at home are left to roam the streets, and many end up on the dump, perishing through disease or malnutrition, sniffing glue to take the edge off their hunger, and joining gangs to survive. It is a wretched existence.

In an extraordinary step which frankly defies any kind of explanation, the Guatemalan government has apparently erected a 'viewing stage' overlooking the city dump so that tourists can observe the communities living at the very edge of existence, with children sieving through the rubbish to find something to eat or to sell. Has the government no sense of shame? Is it proud of how some of its citizens have to live?

We had three hours to kill between arriving back in Guatemala City from Flores and boarding our onward flight to Miami and then to London, so we took a taxi to Zone 1 in the centre of the city, which, according to our guidebook, offered the best of the city. We imagined it would therefore be the safest area to visit, and thought we could kill some time by walking around Parque Central (the central square), and taking a quick look at the presidential palace and the cathedral.

The square is large, overlooked on one side by the Palacio Nacional de la Culture (built in the 1930s and 1940s as a presidential palace but now a museum), and on another by the Catedral Metropolitana (the cathedral built in the late eighteenth century). An ugly hotchpotch of tower blocks and scruffy buildings are built around the rest of the square. We visited the cathedral and wandered across the square, intending to shoot some video footage for the film we had been making for 'José' of all the places we had visited to show him the country of his birth. On one side of the square a group of police, perhaps twelve or fifteen of them, stood under the shade of some trees; on another a few stalls had been set up selling some form of heated meat that looked guaranteed to have you running for the loo. I suggested to Dom that he took some video shots looking down the streets leading from the square, just to give an idea of how busy and scruffy they looked, and he was just getting out his camera when suddenly a gang of ten or so hooded men charged across the street heading right towards where we stood. Now these were not the 'hoodies' that we have in the UK; these were not teenagers out to pick pockets or spray graffiti. These men had great Ku Klux Klan-style hoods over their heads with the eyes cut out, and were carrying fearsome weapons – giant coshes, guns and sticks – and were moving fast in our direction. We have never put away our cameras or moved so fast. They may not have been heading directly for us – a couple of fearful tourists – but make no mistake, they would not have taken kindly to being caught on film, and would have thought nothing of mowing down anyone in their wake. We literally ran across the square and jumped into a taxi, telling the driver to take us to the Marriott Hotel, which we knew to be close to the airport and thought would be a temporary safe haven. As he drove off down one of the streets leading off the main square, the driver paused to let another gang pass in front of our car. This gang numbered at least twenty, all similarly clad in hoods, and carrying an assortment of weapons. We had obviously narrowly avoided being caught in the middle of a bloody showdown.

The driver left us at the hotel and we headed straight for the bar, where we asked the barman for a couple of whiskies. It may have been mid-morning but, shaken by what we had seen, we were in need of a strong drink! Only a month before we travelled to Guatemala we had seen a documentary about the drug gangs of Guatemala City and the high levels of drug-related shootings and murders in the capital. Guatemala has become a major hub for cocaine traffickers moving the substance from Colombia through Mexico to the United States, and it has one of the highest murder rates in Latin America. The documentary painted a vivid picture about how dangerous the city is, and how innocent bystanders are often caught up in the violence, but we had not expected to come across such evidence at ten o'clock on a Thursday morning in Guatemala City's equivalent of Trafalgar Square. Despite the presence of a group of police just on the other side of the square, there they were, huge gangs heading for some massive fight or shoot-out, one we did not have any intention of getting caught up in.

We realised there and then just how dangerous Guatemala City is. We knew now that the adoption agencies had every reason to insist that adoptive parents on visit trips remain in the hotels with their babies; literally not setting foot out of the hotel with their young charges. This was not a city to wander about in, even in the middle of the day.

In just one week we felt we had witnessed some of the best and the worst the country of Guatemala had to offer. We had marvelled at the stunning scenery of lakes and volcanoes in the highlands, and at the verdant green of the jungle in the lowlands; we had been filled with awe at the sight of the magnificent temples erected by the ancient Maya people at Tikal, and had discovered a little of their culture and beliefs; we had wandered through the wonderfully colourful markets and had met many beautiful, friendly Maya. However, we had also seen examples of true poverty and frightening crime; we had seen the impoverished existence of many of the highland Maya families; we had visited abandoned and relinquished children in an orphanage, and had discovered more about the desperate fate of the street children of Guatemala City. We had witnessed the dangers of bandits off the beaten track and of drug gangs in the crime-ridden capital city. It had been a fascinating week; quite a revelation.

Part II
The Waiting Game
(April 2007–March 2008)

9

An Elephantine Gestation Period

10 April 2007

I feel so low at the moment. The euphoria of having passed panel is beginning to evaporate, as we play the endless waiting game. We are obviously relieved and excited that we are now officially eligible to adopt, but everywhere I look, it seems, there are families, children, pregnant women. It is hard not to think about it endlessly, obsessively.

I miss the baby we lost and feel terribly, terribly sad that I will never again experience that amazing euphoric feeling of being pregnant and carrying a new life within me. I feel guilty because I cannot give Dom his own birth child. He always knows when I am down and then when he asks what the matter is and I tell him, I fear that it only serves as a reminder that he will never father a child naturally. I am sure this makes him sad, and feel that if I didn't dwell on it then he wouldn't have to be reminded of our loss and inability to have our own birth child. I feel, too, that this is my fault. If only I was not so old. It is three years now since I got pregnant. It does not seem that long ago. Our little baby would be two years and three months old now, had he or she survived. It is extraordinary how I can miss something – someone – so much when I have never seen him or her. And how much sadness I feel, knowing that I will never again know the joy of being pregnant. I will never give birth to a child. It is what women are meant to do. It is why we are here. All the other women I know have children – or most of them do. I

75

always wanted children. Why did life turn out this way?

I know we both feel the grief – grief at still not being parents. We have friends who were not pregnant when we started this adoption journey, but who have since become pregnant, and even given birth, and still we wait. We are still not a family. It is like a pregnancy with no due date. With a wait of something like two or three years to adopt, this 'gestation period' is truly elephantine. Let's just hope I don't start looking like one!

I must stop wallowing. I shouldn't feel like this. We will have a child. Little 'José' will be every bit as much our child as if I had given birth to him. We are one hundred per cent – no, more like one thousand per cent – determined to adopt a child, to make 'José' a reality. There is absolutely no doubt in my mind that it is what I want to do. What we both want to do. We also know that we will love him every bit as much as we would have loved any birth child. It will make absolutely no difference to us. He will be our child and we will love him unconditionally. I feel it without any doubt; I know Dom feels it too. It is just that in the meantime it is so hard having to wait so long. The path to adoption is so long, so tedious, so gruelling and so tortuous. No wonder so many people give up, dropping by the wayside along the road.

We have just spent the Easter weekend with our families. I love spending time with my sisters and their children. I adore my nephews and nieces, Dom's niece and nephews as well. They are lively, fun, full of energy and enthusiasm. However, it is also hard to be with them when we so want children of our own. When we leave and return home, I just feel so sad that we do not have the families our sisters do. I shouldn't be jealous of them. It will happen to us one day. It is just the waiting that is so hard.

I know Dom feels the same way. We are both a bit low at the moment. So much of our energy went into completing our home-study course and preparing for panel, and now it is frustrating to have to wait so long before we can progress any further. The anti-climax of no activity is immense.

The panel's decision – the approval document – was sent to the

Department for Children, Schools and Families (DCSF) to issue the all-important Certificate of Eligibility, a certificate confirming our eligibility to adopt a baby from overseas. Only at this stage can we proceed further and start applying to Guatemala to adopt.

Apparently the current waiting time for the issue of this certificate is six months. It seems ridiculous that a government department has to take so long merely to rubber-stamp a document so that we can proceed to the next stage.

I must buck up and put a brave face on it all. It upsets Dom when I am down. Last night he was almost in tears at seeing me so upset. He said that he just wants to make me happy and is worried that I am so sad at the moment. I feel terrible. It is not fair of me to make him unhappy. I have so much to be thankful for ... that I have Dom, for a start. I am so lucky to have him as my husband. I could not wish for a kinder, more considerate or more loving partner.

Right, that's it, Alex – stop wallowing. Happy, happy face.

11 April 2007

Never low for long, I have bounced back up again, and I know what does the trick: a bit of voluntary work is good for the soul and helps put a true perspective on life.

A friend recently suggested that Dom and I should consider therapy to help us through our troubles related to trying to conceive and trying to adopt. I have never been one for the therapist's couch, believing that dwelling on and over-discussing one's problems just makes matters worse, leading one to wallow in self-pity. I personally believe a more constructive way of dealing with one's own problems can often be to go and help others. As Julie Burchill once wrote in the *Sunday Times*, 'The therapy culture has brainwashed us into thinking we need help, when if we got off our arses and helped others, we would be helping ourselves, too.' I am sure it doesn't work for everyone, or for every situation, but it often seems to work for me.

I volunteer at a local children's hospice, working as their receptionist and occasionally doing a bit of administration work two afternoons a month, and I really value this time. It is a chance to spend an afternoon with a wonderful group of people who cope with so much and always maintain a cheery outlook. It is a change from dealing with the wealthy and often very demanding clients who provide my bread and butter – grateful though I am to them for providing me with a living – and I find it a real tonic. Whatever troubles I have, I soon realise there are many people out there with far heavier burdens to carry. I return home counting my blessings, with my own problems firmly shoved into perspective.

17 April 2007

We have told my nephews and nieces that Dom and I are planning to adopt a baby from Guatemala. I don't have much experience of children, but I was amazed – and even my sisters were pleasantly surprised – at their responses.

I was babysitting my sister Kate's children and asked them if they remembered seeing the photographs I had shown them of the holiday Dom and I recently took in Guatemala, and if they remembered how poor the conditions were in which some of the families had to live. They nodded emphatically. I told them it was very sad, but some families were so poor that they did not have enough to eat and could not afford to look after all their children, so sometimes they decided it was best to have a child adopted. That way someone else would ensure the child survived, with sufficient to eat and even an education. I then told them that Dom and I had decided that we were going to adopt one of these children, a baby boy, and that it would take a long time but that within the next couple of years they would have a new cousin to play with. I had expected a polite nod to our news before they continued with their meal but instead they were thrilled and excited by our news. Beth, aged twelve, immediately said, 'How cool. That is just so cool.' Amy, aged ten, asked if she could babysit and teach our baby to walk because she just loved babies; and after telling them a little more about how beautiful the children were and how they would have slightly darker skin than we had, little Milly, aged eight, wanted to know the exact shade of brown. 'Will he be the same colour as this chair? Or that table? What colour exactly?'

I then asked my other sister, Susie, if perhaps she would like to tell her boys our news in the same way. I think the way in which they are told is very important, so that in the future the children all have the same perception about our child and why he is with us. At this stage we don't know the exact reason our child will have been put up for adoption, but it is important for the children to understand that in Guatemala poverty is by and large the main reason.

Susie called me back a short while later. She too had expected a rather non-committal response from her children, Felix (aged twelve) and Joe (aged ten). Not a bit of it! Joe's response was similar to Beth's – 'That is such a cool thing to do' – and Felix rather touchingly immediately said that it was a lovely, charitable act and that we could give the child a good education and that his parents would be so very grateful. As he was going to bed that night, Joe asked Susie what she thought it would be like to be adopted – it had obviously made a deep impression on him. The following day when my mother went for a walk with Felix, he immediately asked her if she had heard our news, saying what a nice, charitable thing we were doing. He then added that being so much older he would, of course, have to help and show our son how to do things.

It is very sweet that they think we are doing such a wonderful charitable act, but I know we do not deserve this praise. The really good ones are those who adopt three or four children; children with special needs or older children who have been abused. We, on the other hand, simply would like a family.

At this stage, I think the information and the way we have told them is sufficient. They are a little young to be told all the details surrounding our decision to adopt, though what we have told them is a big part about how we feel and why we wish to adopt from

Guatemala; we do, however, find the 'cool aunt and uncle' impression thoroughly amusing. I have no doubt that this will be the only time we will ever be perceived as being 'cool' by our nephews and nieces.

20 April 2007

I have just faxed one hundred and seven pages (our adoption application form and home-study report) to the agency in America that we are employing to handle our adoption. It seems strange that I have only spoken once to Natasha, the woman who runs the agency – though I have been corresponding with her at length by email and have extensively researched her agency – and yet I have just emailed her every last little detail about us. She has our full home-study report, all the details of our finances, our medicals, our reports written following our preparation course, our views on adoption, life, religion, our experiences of childhood, jobs and relationships, every address we have ever lived at, every detail about our families and details of our closest friends. This woman to whom I have only spoken once on the phone now knows more about us than even my mother, my two sisters and my closest of friends. How bizarre is that? I must admit, it does make me feel rather uncomfortable. It was bad enough that the fourteen members of our adoption panel were party to our innermost thoughts and experiences, but now I have forwarded exactly the same information across the Pond to an agency – to people we do not know. Our lives, it seems, have become public property. I suppose it is a small price to pay that they have to know everything about us, but it still does not sit comfortably.

We did as much research as we could on which agency to use, following up references and contacting couples who had previously used them. We spent the best part of three months poring over information from and about them and the other agencies we considered – but do we know enough? We are about to send them a vast sum of money – the agency and application fee – to begin the process of finding us a child. We are entrusting them with the most important job in the world. They will find us a son. We have to trust them.

We also had to fill in and send to Natasha a form regarding which physical and mental disabilities and other issues we would be prepared to accept in an adopted child. The list was endless and a difficult one to fill in. 'Will you accept a child who is the product of a rape?' 'Will you accept a child who is HIV positive?' 'Will you accept a child whose family has a history of schizophrenia?' 'Will you accept a child who is visually impaired?' 'Will you accept a child with a heart condition?' and so on. We settle on the 'Prepared to consider' box for many of the disabilities and issues rather than a definite 'Will accept' or 'Will not accept', but there were a few categories that we felt unable to accept.

Whilst we are certain we will love any child we are given, whatever its problems, there are certain mental and physical issues that we feel we would perhaps not be able to – or would prefer not to have to – cope with. We had to make some tough decisions and I admit I felt guilty at not agreeing to accept absolutely any child, whatever his disabilities or issues. After all, if you give birth to a child you will love it no matter what disabilities it may have. However, to actively choose to accept a child with a certain disability, problem or background that you know will be a real challenge is not an easy decision to make.

April/July 2007

The months go by ... the wait seems interminable. Every time we see them, family and friends optimistically ask, 'Any news?' It is frustrating that it takes so long. Sometimes I can't help wondering whether it will ever happen.

My sister-in-law, Penny, recently asked me whether a 'Pram-Zimmer combo' might be a useful item for me, by the time our efforts come to fruition. A little tactless perhaps – just as well I have a sense of humour – but it was a funny comment and makes me laugh every time I recall it. She certainly has a point.

It is interesting experiencing the different responses and reactions when you tell people you are planning to adopt. I suppose we will get used to them, and you certainly get all sorts. There is the half-pitying sympathetic nod, behind which you know is, 'Oh dear, poor things. Obviously they can't have their own, so they have to adopt'; then there is the enthusiastic, 'Oh I think that's wonderful; you are so wonderful to do that'; the chill of disapproval: 'Oh? Like Madonna? Mmm . . .', behind which you know they do not like the idea of adoption and certainly not of intercountry adoption. The response I most favour is the simple 'Good luck.'

Many people think ICA is an easy shortcut to getting a family. Can't have your own baby? Never mind, just nip over to a Third World country with a bundle of cash, find an orphanage, choose a baby, pay up, take the child and pop back home again . . . How wrong they are. We are not 'buying' a baby, and this is *not* second best. Adoption is just another way of becoming parents. We are not 'wonderful' to adopt and we do not need sympathy. Support? Yes, we need lots of that on this journey, but sympathy? Certainly not.

Like most couples, we quite simply just want to have a family. Had I been able to conceive again we would have had a birth child and then adopted, but that was not to be and we are excited about, and totally happy with, our decision to adopt a child instead. In addition, we see it as a blessing that we have the opportunity to give a child a future – parents, a home, a loving family, an education – that he would not otherwise have had. There are so many kids on this planet with no one to love them. This is certainly a large part of it, but in the main we just simply want to bring up a child; to have a family.

We are not 'buying' a baby. Yes, it is expensive; cripplingly expensive in fact, but we are paying for *the process*, not for the actual baby. We are paying legal fees for someone to help us with the arrangements – for attorneys in the US and Guatemala to facilitate the process, and for translators, lawyers and notaries in the UK. We are paying for a foster mother to look after our child until the paperwork is complete and we are able to go and pick him up. No one seems to think you are 'buying' a baby if you undergo IVF treatment, and yet what is the difference? They pay a doctor to conduct the medical miracle that is IVF; we pay lawyers to find us a baby and make the arrangements for us to adopt.

How you make a family is not the issue. It is how you live as a family that is important.

I often think of the birth mother of little 'José'. Somewhere in Guatemala there is a woman who is about to give birth, who maybe already has given birth to a little boy she feels unable to keep. I feel incredible empathy with her. I desperately sympathise with her for her situation, and yes, I pity her. What torture is she going through? What pressure is she under? Why is she unable to keep this little boy with her? Poor, poor woman. I cannot imagine what she must be going through. For the past few months, I have been praying for her; praying that somehow she will know that this precious little baby she is unable to keep will be given a good future. That he will be loved. He will be cared for. He will be safe. We do not feel in any way critical of her; we certainly do not blame her. She must have strong reasons, terrible, sad reasons for not being able to keep her son. Perhaps one day we will be able to meet her and tell her how she will always be in our hearts and our thoughts; how grateful we are for the gift she has given us. Our son will always be her son as well, and we will tell him about her. Maybe one day he will be able to meet her again. I just hope she is all right.

Our dossier containing the adoption paperwork is almost in Guatemala now. Once it is in Guatemala our adoption agency in the United States will ask its attorneys in Guatemala to find us a child who has been, or is about to be, relinquished by his birth mother, and refer us.

Over the past month our dossier has travelled from the DCSF to our notary – where we swore our oaths, signed and had it notarised, and where two friends had to swear oaths as our witnesses and to our good characters – and from there to the Foreign Office to be legalised, then to the Guatemalan embassy in London to be legalised, then back to the notary and finally to the DCSF to send out to the British embassy in Guatemala.

Paperwork, paperwork and more paperwork; the paperwork has been endless, and has taken hours, days even, to get together. In addition to the dossier which the DCSF has, we have had to get together additional paperwork to satisfy the authorities in Guatemala – certified copies of our birth certificates, our marriage certificates, and my divorce certificate. We had to write and get notarised an AKA ('also known as') document, ensuring that every possible connotation of our name is included so that nowhere in the dossier are we mentioned by a name not noted on this list. They need photographs – of us, of our extended families, of our friends; a view of the house back and front; of every room of the house; of the future nursery. It seems bizarre. I wonder if there is some clerk sitting in an office in the British embassy in Guatemala looking at our kitchen and asking, 'Um ... space for a high chair? Good. That'll do.' Tick. 'Um ... husband has a kind-looking face. He'll do.' Tick.

I have just started the fifth, yes fifth, file of paperwork. I have so far filled to the brim four large lever-arched files with all the research, paperwork and documents necessary for our adoption. It has taken hours and hours; days and days; months and months; but we are about to enter the most exciting phase. For the last year and a half, I have spent the best part of half a day or often a full day every week researching and working on our adoption. I have neglected my company and work is drying up, but at this moment I don't care. Maybe I should, but all I can focus on is our son. Soon we will have a baby; a son. Soon 'José' will be a reality. I wonder what his real name will be. The anticipation is almost too much for us. We cannot wait.

10

We Have a Son ... a Son We Have Never Met

19 July 2007

I am shaking. I have palpitations. My heart is beating like a drum. I do not know whether to laugh or cry. I am crying. I am laughing. I think I might just have to drown myself in champagne.

It is 8.45 a.m. and I have just switched on my laptop to check my emails and there it is: An innocent little email from the agency in America that is handling the arrangements for our adoption from Guatemala:

'Would you be interested in considering this referral? ...'

WOULD WE BE INTERESTED? We are being referred a little baby! Oh my God ... I cannot believe it. It is actually happening. I am a mother. If nothing goes wrong with this referral – *please God –* then I am now a mother. Dom is a father ... of a son we have never met! ... How surreal is that?

Our agency wants to know if we 'would be interested' in the referral of a little boy. There is not much information, but it is enough.

A baby born in Zacapa, Guatemala on Wednesday, 13 June 2007, weighing 6lb – a very good weight for a Guatemalan baby boy. His birth mother is single, aged 22 years and speaks Spanish. She is a Ladina Guatemalan – i.e. mixed Hispanic and Mayan heritage. He is currently being fostered in Guatemala City. Initial medical tests indicate that he is healthy. They are awaiting further paediatric tests.

That is all we know at the moment. No photo and no further information, except ...

'… He is called José Armando …' *JOSÉ?* How can that possibly be? All along we have been calling our future son 'José', until we knew what name he had been given, and now we are being offered a child actually called José. *It must be meant to be.* It is a sign. This must be our son.

We have other reasons that make us believe that this is fate; that José is meant to be our son. My beloved grandmother, Galli, to whom I was very close, and who died last month, was totally incensed by how long this adoption process was taking. When she died, our adoption paperwork was with the DCSF, awaiting the issue of our Certificate of Eligibility. This stage was currently taking six months and our paperwork had already been there two months so we were not expecting to hear from them until the autumn. A few days after Galli died, we got a letter from the DCSF confirming that our paperwork has been stamped – four months ahead of schedule; the letter is dated 13.06.07 … We have just been offered a referral (i.e. a baby) with a birth date of … 13.06.07!

Galli is obviously sorting all this out for us. She left us, went straight to the Almighty, and I can just hear her saying, 'Now, about this adoption – let's get things moving. First let's get this baby born – and let's call him José as that is what they've been calling him – and furthermore, let's get this paperwork moving.' I'm convinced of it. I can just see her badgering on at God to get it sorted for us.

What's more, 13 June is the feast day of St Anthony – Galli's favourite saint … and the patron saint of all things 'lost and found'. What he has found for us is a son. And 13 June is the date Dom and I met – 13 June 2002 – five years to the very day before little José, our son, was born.

Then there is his name: José, or Joseph in English, has always been my favourite saint, the patron saint of families, and the saint's name I chose for my confirmation.

Need I go on? It just *must* be fate. Thank you Galli.

Jubilant. Ecstatic. Euphoric. The feeling is beyond words. My heart is almost beating out of my chest. This is such an incredible moment. If commencing the process – the interviews, the preparation course – is like conception, conceiving your future child, then the moment of referral is like giving birth – your child has arrived. Am I now giving birth? I almost feel like it!

Why is Dom so far away? Here I am giving birth and where is my husband? On the other side of the world on a business trip in Australia, of all places.

I *must* temper my excitement, but fat chance. We are told not to get too excited yet ... but is that possible? Many first referrals, we are told, do not go ahead. There are a lot of hurdles still.

Believe it or not, we are not even allowed to accept a referral ourselves without acceptance first by the DCSF and our local authority. We have to wait for the laboratory test results to confirm whether the birth mother or the child has any major medical conditions – for example, AIDS/HIV – before our local authority will consider the referral. We have to send these medical test results on to the DCSF and our local authority. They have to check through the details and then meet with us to discuss whether or not we can accept the referral, regardless of whether we ourselves wish to go ahead. Is it really their business? Also, the birth mother could change her mind; could disappear during the process – she has to be interviewed by both the Guatemalan Family Court and the British embassy and at the same time legally relinquish her son for a second time and again sign over her rights. Often birth mums go AWOL and then the adoption cannot go ahead. Also, the birth mother and the child have to have matching DNA to ensure it is the birth mother handing over her own child (essential to guarantee that this is not a case of child trafficking), and so on and so forth ... So we are not there yet ... However – it is just too exciting and I cannot help letting my feelings run away with themselves.

Surely this is the child for us? José, you really *are* called José. You really *are* our child.

23 July 2007

I cannot stop crying. I am sitting at my desk weeping. The emotions are just too much. I have just received some photographs of José from our adoption agency. He is the most beautiful baby I have ever seen. He has chubby cheeks, big dark brown eyes and black hair. His tiny little hands are clenched. He is beautiful; the most beautiful baby in the world. How can I not fall in love with him?

It is torturing me that (a) we do not have the laboratory results and therefore cannot progress and accept this referral; and (b) that Dom is not here to share this moment. It is 4 a.m. in Australia ... I really cannot wake him now... or can I? I text him to call as soon as he awakes and I email the photos on to him in Sydney. I hope he will be able to pick up the attachment and share in this wondrous moment.

Yesterday, Dom told me that he wept on reading the initial offer of referral. He was sitting in the Business Centre at the Hilton Hotel in Sydney blabbing like a baby. A member of the hotel staff came over to check if he was all right. The emotion of it all is getting to us both.

Please God. Please God. Please God, let this be the one. Let the laboratory tests be okay so that we are given the official permission needed to accept this adorable little baby. *Please.*

I can hardly bear it. I am checking my emails every ten minutes, checking to see if the results have come through. Natasha did not want to send the photographs until she had the laboratory-test results in case there is a major problem and we are unable or do not wish to accept the referral, but I persuaded her. She knew we would fall in love with him as soon as we saw his photograph and it would therefore be so much harder for us if we could not accept the referral. She is right – I am in love; in love with the most beautiful little boy in the world. Suppose there is a big medical problem? Suppose it is a major issue and we are recommended not to accept the child? Will we then have to make a decision as to whether we still go ahead even if our child has some dreadful hereditary disease or if

88

he is HIV positive or something else? But even if this is the case, *shouldn't* we still accept? *Can* we still accept? As our local authority needs to give us permission to accept any referral, I can only imagine a further battle and bureaucratic nightmare if we want to accept a referral against their will. Does this child not still deserve a good home, regardless of any problems he may have? At this moment I feel like he is ours already. Surely nothing could persuade us not to accept this referral ...

I have been so blinded by the euphoria of the moment of receiving the referral that I have not stopped to think that anything could be wrong; that maybe we will be advised against accepting the referral. The thoughts are whirling round and round in my head; I pace from room to room; I cannot settle to anything. I know I am working myself up into a ridiculous state when of course the test results will probably be fine. I wish Dom was here. I need him so much at this moment. I cannot bear the suspense. I cannot stop crying. The strain is killing me. Please God let this be okay. Let our little baby be okay. Please. Please. Please. I will be good. I will do anything. *Please.*

3 August 2007

The test results are fine; thank you God. We have now received all the necessary information, and our local authority and the DCSF have given us the go-ahead to accept the referral. Two days ago, on 1 August, Dom (now back from Australia) and I signed the documentation, had it notarised, and have formally accepted the referral. We really do have a son.

We have had a frantic couple of days. We have been unable to do anything before meeting with our local council for them to confirm that we have their permission to accept, and then we have just two days in which to get all the paperwork together before we go on holiday. It is such a rush because Natasha wants our acceptance prior to our holiday, otherwise she has said she will offer the baby to another couple ... *Offer José to someone else?* Over my dead body. However, the formalities in accepting are endless. We have had to get a power of attorney notarised, so that the attorney in Guatemala can act as legal guardian to José on our behalf until the adoption is finalised. This then has to be taken by hand to both the Foreign Office and the British embassy to be stamped, before being sent together with a payment – a cheque, as the Guatemalan banks apparently do not like to accept large money transfers due to drugs-money concerns – by courier to our attorney in Guatemala. At the same time we have signed the adoption acceptance papers and have sent another package by courier, together with copies of the power of attorney papers and cheque, to our agency in the US.

When I go in to the bank to arrange the transaction, having initially been told that they could issue a US cheque there and then, I am now told that they need three days' notice ... but in three days' time we will be away on holiday. A few nervous breakdowns – well, perhaps not exactly, but stress levels are certainly reaching fever pitch – and several phone calls later, and we have arranged for a dear friend to spend the day queuing for us at the Foreign Office and the Guatemalan embassy, and for Dom's boss to receive the cheque, parcel everything up and send the two packages via Fedex – one to the US and one to Guatemala.

Suffice it to say, we most definitely need our holiday.

11

Politics Damn Politics

September 2007

Bit by bit by bit; stage by stage by stage; slowly, slowly, we will get there in the end.

We return from our holiday to another set of photographs and medical details sent by Natasha. Conclusion: a beautiful healthy baby boy. José is so beautiful. We are so lucky; so very, very lucky. We now have a photograph of him in every room. This will have to do until we are able to have him with us for real.

Does the photo make me feel like a mum? Does it make Dom feel like a dad? If I am honest I am not sure. Dom is not sure either. We have certainly fallen in love with the little chap. There is no doubt about that. I knew I loved him from the moment we received his details. We would be devastated if something went wrong and we were not able to bring him home. If his birth mother changed her mind, we would have to try and feel it was best for him to remain in the country of his origin, but we would be devastated. There is certainly a feeling of wanting him with me symbolically all the time, and carrying around his photograph wherever I am makes me feel closer; helps me feel like he is with me night and day. But it does all seem a bit unreal; like a dream; certainly it is very surreal. I am not sure if I can really believe this is happening to us and that I am finally a mother; that Dom is finally a father. I think it will only really seem real once he is here, home with us at last.

It is exciting but frustrating to see the photographs as they arrive

– we have three sets now – and watch him developing and growing without us. I do not want to miss each stage, but we have no choice. We have to wait and be patient. He certainly looks healthy and content. His foster mother, Ilana, is obviously doing a good job and that is a relief. It makes us happy to know he is in safe hands. Natasha seems to be doing a good job for us, too, keeping in contact and sending regular updates and photographs. We just have to hope and pray that the process doesn't take too long; our goal is to have him home at the end of the year or early in 2008. In the very, very worst-case scenario, we *must* have him home before his first birthday, but that is June next year . . . too far away . . . and I am sure he will be with us long before then.

I have completely lost my focus. I cannot concentrate on work. I do not really even care about it at the moment. All I want to do is trawl the Internet sites on adoption and Guatemala.

Meanwhile, the news from Guatemala is very concerning. Casa Quivira, one of Guatemala's foremost *hogars* (orphanages), has been closed down by the authorities last month and the attorneys attached to it have been arrested amid rumours of child trafficking. Within a few days the children have been taken, their formula milk and medicines destroyed and, according to one of the reports I read, the home has been 'turned into a pigpen'. Casa Quivira was the *hogar* that we visited in March. It is inconceivable to me that those wonderful, caring staff should be treated so. It may sound naïve, but I really find it hard to believe that they are involved in child trafficking.

Sure enough, several days later the attorneys have been released and charges against them dropped, but meanwhile the *hogar* remains closed and I gather the owners are still being questioned. And the children? No one knows where they are. Please God they are safe.

Furthermore, and more alarming still, the United Nations is now calling for all intercountry adoptions from Guatemala to be suspended, due to concerns over the process.

There have been reports in the press of child trafficking in

Guatemala and obviously, if these are true and child trafficking is occurring, it needs to be uncovered and stopped. However, many people associated with the adoption situation there – people who know far more about the real situation in Guatemala – are saying that it is misconceptions over the actual process of intercountry adoption there that cause many of these reports on child trafficking and the resulting calls for the suspension of adoptions from Guatemala.

In the *Sunday Telegraph* this month there is a report entitled 'Guatemala's Child-snatching Plague', in which the reporter, Philip Sherwell, writes of babies being stolen and sold for $30,000 to couples adopting internationally, and of birth mothers being paid to hand over their babies. He adds that the UK authorities are so concerned about the adoption procedures that they have reduced the number of adoptions to a trickle – fifty a year. Such reporting is full of mistruths and is damaging to the reputation of intercountry adoption, to those who adopt from overseas, and most importantly of all, to the children who are adopted from Guatemala.

I write a letter to the editor of the *Sunday Telegraph* to complain, as do many others involved in intercountry adoption who know the facts of the situation far better than I do. Britain has not reduced adoptions from Guatemala to a trickle because of concerns, as they reported. The number has always been way below this fifty a year. The highest ever number of applications for adoption from Guatemala to England – not completed adoptions – was twenty-nine, in 2003. The actual adoptions seen through to completion will have been well below even this number. The number of adoptions has not been reduced due to any concerns about procedures. The numbers are already low, and that is due to a variety of other factors, not because of concerns over the procedures in Guatemala.

Babies are *not* priced at thirty thousand dollars. Those adopting from Guatemala pay a fee to the attorneys to make the adoption arrangements. The fee is for legal services and to cover the costs of a foster mother to care for the child until the adoption is completed, not for the baby, and the birth mother is not paid for passing over her baby. If a baby has been snatched it would not be possible for the baby to be subsequently adopted into the US or the UK. All adoptions require DNA matching between birth mother and child to ensure that the child is indeed the birth child of the woman handing him or her over. Finger- and foot-printing further ensure against child trafficking. In addition, the birth mother has to be extensively interviewed by the Family Court and the embassy. If either body has any concerns about the birth mother being coerced into giving up her child or being paid, or if the DNA does not match, then the case is immediately closed and the adoption is not processed.

The lawless situation in many parts of Guatemala and the fate of many of the children there is of huge concern, but incorrect articles in the press do not help and merely add further fuel to the argument that adoptions should be suspended. What then would be the fate of the children whose mothers cannot keep them due to poverty or their own personal situations?

The presidential election is due to be held in Guatemala later this month and we will wait with bated breath to hear the new president's policy on adoption. President Berger, the outgoing president, has supported the move against intercountry adoptions and many of the candidates follow his view. Who knows what the next president will do?

Please God, good common sense will prevail and the authorities will not give in to these largely unsubstantiated rumours.

10 September 2007

The presidential election was held in Guatemala yesterday. There were fourteen candidates but none received the fifty per cent majority needed and there will now be a run-off. The two candidates with the most votes – Alvaro Colom (a businessman) and Otto Perez Molina (a former general) – will go through to a second election to be held at the beginning of November.

During the presidential campaign, more than fifty candidates, activists and their relatives were murdered. Guatemala needs a good firm hand; a leader who can start to tackle the corruption and poverty in the country. I pray that whoever wins is up to this task.

22 September 2007

Excited. Nervous. Terrified. Happy. Impatient. Frustrated. Worried. Ecstatic. Every emotion is experienced as the weeks go by and we slowly progress through the adoption process.

We received new medicals and photographs from Natasha this week. José really is such a beautiful little boy. Such big brown almond-shaped eyes. You could sink into them for ever. I bet the girls will be after him in a few years – not for quite a few years yet though, I hope. Medically, everything seems to be in order, which is fantastic. He is small. A little small for his age, but that is not unusual for a Guatemalan baby and we are urged not to be unduly concerned.

A DVD has also arrived ... oh my God; what an absolute darling. To see him for the first time moving, yawning, blinking, staring round the room and at his foster mother was the most unbelievable experience. It had me in tears, of course. Dom was moved too. I wanted to stroke the TV just to be nearer him. I cannot wait; we cannot wait, for that first moment when we can hold him in our arms. It is hard not to obsess about it all the time. I think of him every day, almost every hour. I am willing the process on. Please God, do not let anything upset our case.

27 September 2007

There is so much uncertainty in this whole process. It is hard to stay on an even keel. We feel we have a son. That it is only a matter of time before we can bring him home ... and yet ... First, his birth mother has not even had her British embassy interview yet, nor had her DNA taken. What if the DNA is not a match? Our adoption case would grind to a halt, for the child would not be hers to relinquish. What if she fails to turn up for her interview? Again, we would not be able to adopt José. What if she changes her mind and decides to keep her son? Again, no son for us. These are not unusual scenarios. Every time we meet other adoptive parents or go online on to the various adoption support groups that we have joined, we come across families going through one or other of these nightmare scenarios.

In addition, there is the uncertainty over the whole political situation of adoptions in Guatemala. Yesterday the US Department of State issued a statement – a warning – urging American citizens not to commence the adoption process in Guatemala at this time. It states that fundamental changes in Guatemalan and US adoption law that will be taking place over the next six months are likely to inject considerable uncertainty into the adoption process. This is all to do with the knock-on effect of Guatemala becoming a Hague Convention country on 1 January 2008.

The Hague Adoption Convention is a 'Convention on the Protection of Children and Co-operation in Respect of Intercountry Adoption'. It is a multilateral treaty that includes a large number of countries worldwide, and its goal is to protect children, birth parents and adoptive parents involved in intercountry adoption and to prevent child trafficking and other abuses. The Convention sets internationally agreed procedures for the countries who participate in intercountry adoption.

In order for Guatemala to fall in line with the Hague requirements, certain changes to the adoption laws will need to be made. We just have to hope that any changes will not disrupt the progress of our case.

Dear God, please let everything be all right. Please let us bring our son home, without too many delays. He needs a good home; he needs a loving family. We can offer him a home and a family, and he will certainly never want for love.

28 September 2007

The Guatemalan president, Oscar Berger, has just announced plans to suspend all intercountry adoptions from Guatemala with American families as of 1 January 2008. *He also calls for the suspension of all adoptions currently in process.*

Most adoptions of Guatemalan children by British couples are handled via American agencies, and hence if American adoptions are suspended, it is likely that adoptions from Guatemala to England will be suspended as well.

I have been in tears all day. I just do not know which way to turn. What can we do? Surely this will not – cannot – happen?

There are apparently approximately 5,000 children – including our little José – currently 'in process' (that is, they have been 'referred' to potential adoptive parents, accepted and are awaiting finalisation of the paperwork before they can go to their new homes). The birth parents of these children have already relinquished their parental rights. The Guatemalan government does not have enough orphanages – in terms of finances or facilities – for these children. If adoptions are suspended these children will literally have no place to go and may well end up on the street like the thousands of other homeless Guatemalan children.

One in every one hundred Guatemalan babies born each year is adopted by a family in the United States. Last year Americans adopted 4,135 Guatemalan children, second only to the number they adopted from China. If these adoptions are stopped, since there is virtually no domestic adoption in Guatemala, what will happen, not only to the children already in process, but also to the thousands of children who will be born next year, the year after and the year after that, whose birth parents for one reason or another, largely poverty, cannot keep them? They too will have nowhere to go.

The president's proposed plan – the Berger Plan, or the Ortega Bill, as it is called – really is a crisis waiting to happen.

I cannot even begin to get my head around the fact that this could prevent us from bringing José home. Surely that won't happen.

Surely we can find a way to bring our son home. Although my feelings of panic are mounting, I am in denial that this could possibly happen.

What can we do? Adoption agencies and parents across America are besieging their US Senators, the US House of Representatives, the Department of State Office of Children's Issues and UNICEF, asking them to get involved and imploring the president of Guatemala *at the very least* to ensure all adoptions in process be allowed to proceed to completion.

Thousands of people across America, and now across the United Kingdom as well, are signing a petition to the DOS (the US Department of State) and to the US president, and another one to UNICEF, to put pressure on them to ensure the in-process cases at the very least can proceed. I have sent an email to everyone I know – family, friends, clients – imploring them to sign the petitions, but what else can we do?

I feel completely desperate. What will happen to José if we cannot bring him home? Can we not speed up the process so that it is completed before January, before this bill comes into effect? Realistically, though, there is little we can do. We are at the mercy of the politicians.

I have been trying to ring our agency. No reply. Understandable, I suppose; I expect they are being inundated with calls from all the other equally desperate PAPs.

Please God, do not let adoptions be suspended in Guatemala. *Please God*, let us bring José home.

4 October 2007

Bad news: the Ortega Bill was apparently passed yesterday. Although it is not actually intended to stop intercountry adoptions altogether but is implementing legislation regarding these adoptions, it is likely to be so restrictive that the actual result will be that intercountry adoptions cannot continue, at least for the foreseeable future.

Furthermore, for quite some time, the government in Guatemala has wanted to find a way to take adoptions out of the hands of agencies and lawyers, who they perceive to be making too much money and in some cases to be corrupt, and to place adoption arrangements into the hands of their own courts and adoptions council. There are apparently somewhere in the region of six hundred private attorneys in Guatemala participating in the adoption business, and many believe they do make a disproportionate amount of money from each and every adoption. However, the problem is that Guatemala's courts are so notoriously slow that it is believed that if adoptions are taken away from private attorneys then the already lengthy adoption process will take so much longer that potential adoptive parents will feel forced to look to other countries to adopt.

On 9 October the Guatemalan Congress will sit again to discuss the question of whether there are to be any clauses in the implementation of this new bill and the possibility of postponement of its actual implementation. We have to hope for a 'grandfathering clause' – that is, a clause allowing those cases in process, including ours, to be grandfathered through (allowed to proceed).

I have written a letter to Cardinal Cormac Murphy-O'Connor (head of the Roman Catholic Church in England and Wales), which is apparently going to be passed to the Bishops' Conference department that handles international cases such as these. I have stressed that there are just a couple of working days left in which to act. I have also got the contact details (that took a while!) of the Cardinal of Guatemala, and have written and faxed him a letter. Guatemala is a Catholic country, after all, so pressure from either cardinal could have an effect. Anything is worth a go.

I have spoken today to our agency. Natasha thinks that it *may* still be possible that the British cases in process will be allowed through and that this law may only affect the US cases. *May* be possible? 'May' is not good enough. We need a definite 'Yes' and we will not rest until we have got one. Natasha, together with Pedro, our attorney in Guatemala, are working really hard to try and get all their cases completed by the end of the year just in case the worst happens and the in-process cases aren't allowed to proceed. God willing, our case will be completed by the end of the year and we will have José home before the implementation of this new law in January 2008.

Dom and I discuss this situation incessantly every evening when he gets back from work. We lurch from denial about the severity of the situation and optimism that surely nothing will prevent us bringing José back, to despair and tears at the thought that the politicians could prevent our little boy coming home.

We have been considering every possible means to bring Jose home. Would ringing the British embassy in Guatemala make a difference? Should we get the British government involved? Have we gone high enough in the Church? Perhaps we should contact the papacy? What about letting the press know? Can we deal direct with our attorney and get our case through quicker? Could we bribe someone? Anyone? (Only joking ... but only just!) Could we just go there and smuggle him across the border into Mexico? Somehow I cannot quite see us as Bonnie and Clyde fugitives. We will try anything, but breaking the law – English or Guatemalan – is not going to be the answer. We do not want José to be an illegal immigrant unable to ever have a passport; nor do we want to end up in jail – that really would not help anyone.

I could not survive without Dom at the moment. He is such a comfort, so strong for me, for us both, and yet I know he is as upset and worried as I am. We must remain strong; we will remain strong. We will find a way to bring José home. There is absolutely no question of us giving up. Never ... Never ... *Never.*

11 October 2007

What a couple of weeks it has been. Tensions are running high both at home and in the intercountry adoptive community at large.

As far as the political situation is concerned, regarding the suspension of intercountry adoptions from Guatemala, the ghastly, tense situation continues. Although the Ortega Bill was passed last week, thus legally suspending intercountry adoptions from Guatemala into the United States as of 1 January 2008, amendments to the law are still to be discussed by the Guatemalan Congress sometime in November. Originally planned for 9 October, this discussion has now apparently been postponed until after the second round of the presidential election and probably will not be heard until mid-November.

The Joint Council on International Children's Services (JCICS) is calling for a clause (amendment) in this bill to allow the five thousand transition cases (i.e. those adoption cases that are in process) to be seen through to completion. At this stage there is still no news on whether adoptions from Guatemala to England will be allowed to continue or whether the ban will include all overseas adoptions from there. There seems to be a difference of opinion in the adoption community on this subject, and there is no official word from the British embassy in Guatemala. As the majority of in-process cases are destined for the United States, we have been advised not to draw attention to the British cases by contacting any official bodies in Guatemala – otherwise we would have called the British embassy for clarification. So the terrible uncertainty continues.

Regarding our personal adoption case, we wait with bated breath for news of our birth mother's interviews. Maria, José's birth mother, had her interview at Family Court yesterday, and today she will be interviewed at the British embassy. These interviews are to establish that she is giving up José of her own free will and is not being paid any money for this relinquishment. The interviews are very strict and very difficult, particularly for a young, uneducated woman who has probably seldom been far from her own village, and apparently they often leave the birth mothers in tears. I feel for her and have been praying that she is all right and that she can cope with the stress of the situation and does not find it too upsetting.

Maria will also have her DNA taken at the British embassy, as will José. The DNA samples will be sent to the UK for a laboratory to verify they are a match and that Maria is indeed his birth mother and therefore in a position to relinquish José for adoption. I pray too that the DNA is a match and that we can proceed with the adoption of our little son. The alternative is not worth contemplating.

Pedro will have collected Maria from her village and taken her to both interviews, arranging for her to be put up in Guatemala City overnight. It may well be her first visit to the city.

It will take two to three weeks to get the results of the DNA tests, and then, providing they are a match, we will be able to go out and meet José. We cannot wait. We have been strongly advised not to travel out before the birth mother's interviews and before we have these results (though of course we wanted to get on the next flight to see him when we accepted the referral back in August), in case there is a problem and either the DNA does not match and/or Maria changes her mind at one or other of the interviews and decides to keep him.

Once the British embassy has the DNA results, providing it is happy with the interview, it will pass our case. At the same time, hopefully, our case should have exited Family Court and it should then be able to be sent to the PGN (Procuraduria General de la Nacion). This is the Attorney General's office, the final court approval stage in the adoption of a child from Guatemala.

Natasha expects our case to enter PGN by mid-November, providing there are no hitches along the way. If we are really lucky she thinks there is a chance that we may complete by the end of the year or sometime in January. Could we get our little son home before the beginning of January, before the new law comes into effect? It is a long shot and, realistically speaking, it is unlikely, but we can hope.

Pedro is apparently intending to try and speed our case through Family Court with constant calls to the woman responsible for our case. Unlike many of the attorneys, he apparently will not consider monetary bribing . . . though frankly, at this stage, it is tempting to try and persuade him to consider anything.

However, on the political front, the really good news is that *petitions do work!* Within twenty-four hours of the first petition – the one to the DOS and the US president – going online, the DOS altered its position, announcing that it would back transition cases. This petition now has more than 39,000 signatures and we understand that the US Congress is finally waking up to and discussing the problem.

The second petition to UNICEF has been growing more slowly but does now have more than 11,800 signatures. A couple of days ago, UNICEF put out the following announcement: 'UNICEF urges national authorities to ensure that, during the transition to full implementation of the Hague Convention, the best interests of each individual child are protected.' This revised position of UNICEF is a very positive move, despite not going as far as we would like – but the adoptive community and JCICS is still putting the pressure on UNICEF to issue a further revised and more clear statement of support for a clause to allow the five thousand in-process cases to be completed.

I have today written a letter to UNICEF, adding my voice to the thousands of others petitioning them for further action, and I am still campaigning to get the Catholic Church involved.

Having contacted Cardinal Cormac Murphy-O'Connor last week, I went to speak to my parish priest on Saturday, telling him of the problem. I was hoping that he would perhaps add his voice to mine in urging Cardinal Cormac to get involved to save the plight of these five thousand children who will have no homes to go to if their adoptions are not allowed to proceed.

Instead he suggested that I spoke to the parishioners at the three masses over the weekend. That way, he felt, I could appeal to between four and five hundred people to sign the petitions. Speaking in front of so many people is a rather alarming prospect, but if it helps, anything is worth a go. We agree it would be better if I did not mention José or the fact that we were personally trying to adopt from Guatemala, but just left it as an appeal on behalf of the five thousand children. Although to Dom and me, José is the most important little person in the world, this is a far larger crisis involving thousands of children and it is on behalf of all these children that I must appeal.

I wrote a speech and read it out to all the parishioners at the various masses at our church on Sunday. Our parish priest very kindly photocopied four hundred copies of a petition notice giving details of the online links to the petitions. My speech read as follows:

Crisis for the Children of Guatemala

A humanitarian crisis is about to occur for the children of Guatemala. I am asking for your assistance in trying to avert this crisis.

Guatemala, in Central America, is one of the poorest countries in the Americas and many children are abandoned or relinquished by their parents, often due to poverty. 4,000 to 5,000 children live on the rubbish dump on the outskirts of Guatemala City and 25,000 to 30,000 children live in orphanages.

A small percentage of these children are adopted by families in the United States and fewer still by families in the UK and other countries.

Ten days ago the Guatemalan president, Oscar Berger, announced plans to suspend intercountry adoption from Guatemala as of 1 January 2008. He has also called for the suspension of all adoptions currently in process.

There are currently approximately 5,000 children 'in process' – that is, the birth parents of these children have already relinquished their parental rights and they have adoptive homes waiting for them in the US and a few in the UK. The Guatemalan government does not have enough orphanages – finances or facilities – for these children. If adoptions are suspended these children will literally have no place to go and will end up languishing in orphanages or most likely, worse still, on the streets.

The final reading and vote on this law takes place in the Guatemalan Congress on 4 November. This law, the Ortega Law, has been heavily influenced by UNICEF. If passed, it will mean that intercountry adoption becomes virtually impossible in Guatemala, as it has in other Central and South American countries, including Peru, Honduras and El Salvador. Stopping adoptions in these countries has not resulted in any benefits for the children and families there.

The UNICEF position is that children should have the right to live in their own country and be brought up in their own culture. In fact, in Guatemala, for many children, denying them the opportunity to be adopted overseas means that their actual right is to die on the rubbish dump. Many of the children of the poor Mayan Indian families die from malnutrition. To suggest that they could be adopted by other family members (who are equally poor), as UNICEF do, is ridiculous, and completely impossible. There is virtually no domestic adoption in Guatemala as middle-class Latin families do not adopt poor Mayan children, so intercountry adoption is the only chance for these children to survive.

It is the futures, the lives even, of thousands of abandoned and relinquished children in Guatemala that are at stake.

The Joint Council on International Children's Services strongly opposes such a suspension and has asked for support worldwide in their efforts to ensure that all children retain the right to a permanent home and a safe future through intercountry adoption.

There are two petitions that we have been urged to sign, one calling on the President of the United States for his involvement, and the other to UNICEF. These petitions are online and I will be handing out details as you leave mass.

At the very least, we need to ensure that there is a clause included in any bill passed by Guatemalan Congress that allows the 'grandfathering' of the in-process cases – that is, to allow those cases 'in process' to be completed so that these 5,000 children can go to the permanent adoptive homes they have already been found.

I urge you please to go online and sign these petitions.

In addition, and also for those of you who do not have access to computers, we ask for your prayers for the children of Guatemala.

Thank you for your time and for listening.

It was rather alarming to have to stand up and read out the speech at all four of the weekend services. I was terrified and shaking like a leaf at the first mass, but less so at the second. By the third mass, I was actually quite enjoying it – perhaps I am a campaigner at heart – next stop a soapbox at Hyde Park Corner?

The response from the parishioners was tremendous. As they left the church, all but two people asked for notices with the online link for the petition.

I received a very nice email back from Cardinal Cormac Murphy-O'Connor yesterday (in response to my letter sent last week), thanking me for alerting him to the situation. Furthermore, having gone online to the various Guatemalan support groups here and in America that we have joined to tell them of my actions in the hope that others would follow suit, I have received several requests for copies of my letters to the cardinals so that others can write similar letters to Cardinal Cormac and also to cardinals in America. I have also received several requests for my speech from other adopters interested in getting their churches involved as well.

We *think* things are *very slowly* moving in the right direction. Of course the Guatemalan Congress may choose to ignore the pressure from the DOS, JCICS and UNICEF (if we do manage to get full UNICEF support), but we have to continue to do what we can to keep the pressure up.

I really am turning into a right campaigner – at the expense of my work, my business and the housework, but if it is a question of priorities, well, frankly, no contest. We will not stop until we get José home.

The support we are receiving from families, friends and even my clients is tremendous. Just about everyone I know has gone online to sign the petitions. A friend of my sister Kate has even translated my email appeal into Spanish so she could send it home to her family and friends in Ecuador; Kate and her sister-in-law have sent it to all the mothers of the children in their classes at school; Susie, my other sister, has also written to our cardinal, and my mother has written to a bishop she knows, and has just about the entire Catholic community (slight exaggeration, but only just!) in England praying for us. There are people right across the country praying for José and a successful outcome to our adoption. People I do not even know are praying for us and for our little boy. It makes me feel quite humble and incredibly grateful.

If goodwill, prayers and positive thoughts win through, we will succeed. Either way, *we will not give up* until we have José safely home with us.

13 October 2007

Some good news at last: We heard this morning that both Maria's interviews – at the British embassy and at the Family Court – went well. Thank you Maria. We will always be so grateful to her for giving us this chance to become a family, and can only hope that she is coping with this difficult period. To say that it cannot have been easy giving up a child she has carried for nine months is such an understatement, and I often wonder how she is coping with this loss. Although we do not yet know the circumstances of her pregnancy or reasons that she feels she has to give up José, I am certain such a decision must have been terribly difficult to make.

We have learnt that Maria named José herself and spent three days with him in hospital before giving him to Ilana, our foster mother. We are due to go and visit José next month and will be able to have him stay with us for three days, the same length of time that Maria spent with him. I am already dreading having to give him back and returning home without him, but we are optimistic that our parting will be temporary. How much harder must it have been for Maria, carrying him for nine months, giving birth to him and then caring for him for those three short days? Such a bittersweet time they will have had together. Whilst I will always be grateful to her for the chance she has given me to become a mother, part of me will always feel sad for her that she had to make this choice.

The interviews are the stage at which some birth mothers change their minds. Maria did not, or could not perhaps, because of her circumstances. Her tragic loss is our wonderful gain.

The DNA samples taken from Maria and José at the British embassy are now on their way in the diplomatic bag to a laboratory in England, where they will be tested to ensure they are a match. Only once this is established can we progress. We eagerly await the results.

25 October 2007

Alleluia! Whilst we never doubted that the DNA would be a match, the excitement and relief we felt on actually receiving confirmation is amazing. The DNA profiling report arrived today. It gives Maria 'a relative chance of maternity of 99.998 per cent compared with a random-selected individual'. The report goes on to state that a female first-degree relative (i.e. mother, sister or daughter) would have a relative chance of maternity of 1.959 per cent compared with Maria. Well, I think that is pretty conclusive.

The DNA results have been faxed back to the British embassy, which will now hopefully be able to confirm agreement to our adoption and release the paperwork. Meanwhile we await the exit of our case from Family Court (the Guatemalan side of the proceedings) so that it can enter PGN, the final court stage in Guatemala.

I really feel that there is no stopping us now. Our adoption case can proceed and we can now *finally* go out and meet our son.

Whilst our individual adoption case is progressing well, we still do not really know for certain about the political situation regarding the suspension of adoptions and how it will affect us. Conflicting statements have been appearing on the various websites. The JCICS website says President Berger is not supporting the completion of in-process cases, whilst the Guatadopt.com website says Berger has agreed to allow the in-process cases through. Both websites are usually reliable sources of information and I can only think that Berger must have made a perhaps somewhat vague statement that has been misinterpreted by one or other of the sources. It is *so* frustrating. This lack of clear information is driving us insane. Furthermore, we still do not even know if England will be affected by this ban. It should not be. We are part of the Hague Convention, and if adoptions to the United States are being suspended because the United States is not Hague compliant, this should not affect adoptions to England. On the other hand, our arrangements have been made via the United States. Ninety-five per cent of adoptions from Guatemala go to the United States, so maybe Congress has just not considered the remaining five per cent. Maybe the suspension is meant for all cases and we will be prevented from bringing our son home if the grandfathering clause is not included. On the other hand, maybe the British cases can slip through the net, as there are so few of them.

We live in hope. We have to remain positive, but it is just so frustrating. We are desperately worried and the strain is beginning to show. Both Dom and I are struggling to cope and yet we are convinced that it will work out. Maybe we are being overly optimistic or, more likely, we simply cannot contemplate the alternative. We *will* bring José home, and we *will* bring him home soon.

As I sit typing at my desk, a picture rests on the windowsill in front of me. It is a picture of José taken in August when he was just ten weeks old. He is staring directly into the camera. Those huge almond-shaped dark brown eyes look at me as if to say, 'I trust you. I am not worried. I know you will come for me. I know you will find a way and I will soon be home with you.' It is those eyes – those trusting eyes – that keep me going.

Meanwhile, now that the DNA samples are confirmed a match, we can book a visit to meet our José, who can come and stay with us at our hotel for a few days. In common with many of the adoption agencies, ours allows a brief visit trip such as this. Any longer would cause too much disruption to the baby's schedule.

We go in a couple of weeks' time. I cannot wait; we cannot wait. We are so very excited. We are about to meet our son.

12

Meeting Our Son ... at Five Months Old

13 November 2007: Awaiting our first visit to José

I feel physically sick; sick with excitement. My stomach is cramped. I am breathless and fear an asthma attack. Dom is feeling the same. We have less than twenty-four hours to go before we meet our son for the very first time. The excitement is almost too much for us. José will be brought to the Guatemala City Marriott Hotel, where we are staying, and will be left with us for three days, before we will have to return him to his foster mother and come home without him, whilst the remainder of the adoption process is completed.

We arrived at the Marriott last night. Nicknamed 'Baby Central' by locals, it is the hotel that is used by most adoptive couples on their visit trips when they meet the children they are adopting, and on the pick-up trips when they are finally reunited and can take them home. The Marriott is an ugly, modern 1970s-style block from the outside, with rather alarming Guantanamo Bay-type fencing (high and with an abundance of barbed wire) surrounding it. On the inside, however, the hotel gives the impression of a pretty regular four-star business establishment – nicely decorated and with every facility the business traveller could require – until you look a little closer and realise that this is not the standard Marriott business hotel that you find in just about every capital city in the world. Along the corridors, in the restaurants, round the pool pace weary, pale-faced, cooing couples cradling and feeding beautiful little coffee-coloured babies. They are everywhere you look. It is a surreal sight; like something out of movie where everything looks normal on the face of it and then the more you look the more you realise the scene is not quite as it seemed.

At first glance the other parents all look so in control, like they know what they are doing. We feel so inadequate at this stage. My best friend and one of my sisters have both given me a crash course in baby care – how to feed and bath a baby and how to change a nappy – but I still feel like I don't know what I am doing. I so want this visit to go well. I certainly do not want to alarm or scare our little son. It is so important that his first experience of us, his parents, is a good one.

We had been advised not to buy bottles, teats or formula feed in advance in England. Apparently they are so different in Guatemala that it is better to buy locally or our baby may reject our attempts to feed him. So, first thing this morning we decided to get ourselves sorted out and buy these vital items. Where is the nearest pharmacy? What type of formula should we get? The concierge was able to give us all this information. 'What age is your son, madam?' he asks. I tell him five months old. 'Ah, you'll be wanting NAN2 then, madam. I suggest one large tub and four or five bottles should be sufficient for your stay.' I am impressed, and highly amused. Where else in any hotel in the world would your hotel concierge be able to tell you not only what brand of formula you should buy, but also what level? This really is a strange experience.

We may well get cabin fever during our stay. For security reasons we are not allowed out of the hotel when José is with us. Guatemala is not a safe city, to put it mildly, and white couples with Guatemalan babies are an easy target for the police, who have a reputation for being both corrupt and heavy-handed. We have been told that they would almost certainly stop us, and without our adoption papers (we will not have those until the adoption process is completed), they would take our little son away. Babies taken by the police are rarely seen or heard of again. One does not even want to begin to think what happens to them. So remaining within the hotel is the sensible option. Unfortunately it doesn't have a garden, so the small area around the outdoor swimming pool will provide our only fresh air – but what the hell, it is only for a few days. Cabin fever is a small price to pay to be with our son.

Our bedroom is a standard hotel room size; not bad, but with our bed, a cot and all the baby paraphernalia we seem to have accumulated there is not much space. We do have two windows though. One overlooks the ugly concrete jungle that is much of this city. The only notable landmark, if you can call it that, is the golden arches of a McDonald's sign – is there a city in the world without one? The other window overlooks a six-lane highway along which career, at breakneck speed, trucks and the clapped-out old Chicken Buses. They are often crammed way beyond capacity, with passengers hanging from the doors, windows and sometimes even the roof, on which luggage and broken boxes are piled high. They have a fearful reputation for causing accidents as they charge round corners and weave through traffic, honking their horns and belching out thick black smoke. They seem to be held together, and to remain on the road, by sheer willpower alone.

A conversation with our concierge reminds us of the security problems in the city and reassures us that our adoption agency is right to tell us we have to remain within the four walls of the hotel compound. Dom mentioned in passing to the concierge at the front desk the noisy sound of the Chicken Buses backfiring on the highway outside the hotel. 'No sir. I am afraid that is the sound of gunfire, not Chicken Buses. It would be best to remain in the hotel when you hear that noise.' I think we will happily put up with cabin fever during our stay.

Sorting ourselves out for the all-important arrival of our son, our first attempts at preparing a feed are a joke. Such is the incompetence of us as first-time parents that somehow it manages to take us two hours just to sterilise and make up four bottles of formula. Oh dear – this way we are going to have to have one of us permanently on bottle duty whilst the other tends to our little chap.

We meet an American couple in the bar for a drink. They are adopting via the same agency and we have been corresponding by email. They are friendly and equally nervous about their visit trip. 'Thank goodness this is our second child, although our first adopted one,' one of them says. 'I can't imagine how parents cope with this when it is their first time.' Mmmm ...Well, at least we have their sympathy, I suppose.

14 November 2007: Day one of our first visit to José – six hours after meeting our son for the first time

Most mothers are naked and sweaty when they meet their babies for the first time. I, on the other hand, was wearing a new dress. Red, blue and yellow flowers ... young children like primary colours, don't they? Cotton ... easily washable in case my son took one look at his new mother and promptly threw up all over me.

We were excited, so very excited; and nervous, very, very nervous. The moment we had waited for so, so long had finally arrived. There was a knock on our hotel bedroom door, and there standing in the doorway were two women – Ilana, José's foster mother, and Ana, our agent's representative who was acting as interpreter. In Ilana's arms lay the cutest, most adorable, exquisitely beautiful little baby I had ever seen.

Words are completely inadequate to describe my feelings at that moment – the moment I finally set eyes on my son.

As Ilana walked in carrying our little boy, he turned his head to look up at me and I was immediately struck by his eyes – large, dark brown almond-shaped pools which seemed to stare right into my very being. 'Oh, you're beautiful, so beautiful. Oh, you're so very beautiful,' was all I could say, over and over again. I could not take my eyes off him. I struggled with my emotions. I wanted to cry.

There followed a rather surreal scene as the four of us – Ilana, still clutching José (would she ever hand him over?), Ana, translating our conversation, my husband and I – sat perched on the edge of our bed and on a couple of chairs, in the somewhat cramped conditions of our hotel room, making polite small talk about our son, his likes and dislikes, whether we had had a good flight, and, of all irrelevant facts, the current weather in England. All I wanted to do was grab José, usher our guests out and be alone with my husband and, at last, our son.

We discussed a few details regarding José's care – his routine ('He doesn't have one'); what he eats ('Still on formula milk except for a little apple or carrot purée once a day'); how often ('Formula every two hours night and day' – ah well, there goes any sleep); how best to comfort him when he cries ('Oh, he doesn't cry; he just screams ... when he is happy as well as when he is sad') – and still Ilana sat there with José on her lap.

The temptation to snatch him from her was almost irresistible. Bizarrely though, it did not seem the right thing to do. For the moment at least, his foster mother was the one acting as his mother. We had to take our lead from her.

Finally, after what seemed an eternity, the interpreter turned to me and said, 'Would you like to hold him now?' Would I? I have never moved so fast.

At last, at long, long last, I was holding our son in my arms. My little baby boy. The euphoria of that moment will remain with me for ever. Even writing now, my eyes well up at the memory.

Five hours later and José was still screaming; poor little mite. His foster mother, the woman he had known as his mother since he was just three days old, had left; left him with a couple of pale-faced strangers, awkward and ham-fisted, not knowing what he wanted and when. No wonder he was distressed.

I had prayed long and hard that this moment would not be too alarming for him, that we would not scare him. At the moment at least, it appeared our prayers were going unheeded.

He eventually settled, sobbing himself to sleep on my chest as I sat in a chair rocking him; trying to soothe his distress. It was the most extraordinary feeling – the complete relaxation and trust of his little body in my arms, just like a long, long hug.

We studied him as he slept. He is tiny – much smaller than I had imagined. Although he is five months old he weighs only twelve

March 2007, Guatemala

Above: Visiting Guatemala for the first time. Dom and me at Lake Atitlan in the Highlands.

Below: Arco de Santa Catalina in Antigua, the former colonial capital of Guatemala.

March 2007, Guatemala

Left: Typical Maya home, in Concepcion in the Highlands.

Below: The colourful market at Chichicastenango.

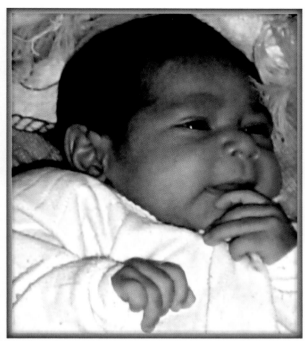

July 2007

Left: "Are you interested in the following referral?..."
First photograph received of our son (aged 5 weeks).

November 2007
Guatemala: first visit to meet our son, aged 5 months

Below: Holding José in my arms for the first time.

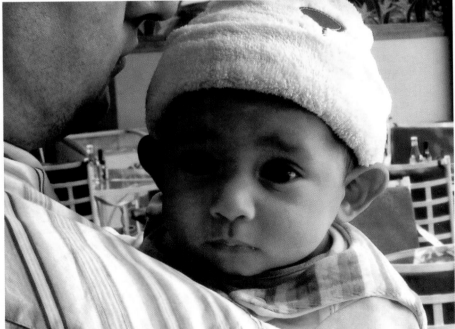

November 2007, Guatemala

Above: First family photograph.

Below: Last day of our first visit to meet José. How can we possibly say goodbye?

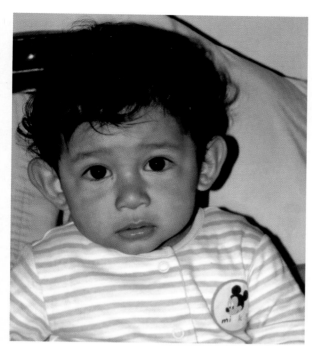

May 2008, Guatemala. The "pick-up" trip

Left: Day 2 with his new parents: Bewildered by all the changes.

Below: Our first few days as a family in Guatemala before the long journey home.

May 2008

Above: Guatemala. Fortune shines on us: we are there to witness José's first few steps.

Below: Heathrow Airport. The happiest moment of my life: our arrival on English soil with José.

Home in England

Above: June 2008. Back home and happily beginning to bond with Mummy.

Below: March 2009. On holiday in Dorset. Enjoying the ride with Daddy.

March 2009, England

Left: José sits in the Judge's chair at Court - after the final hearing on our adoption of José in England – with his parents and grandparents. After 3½ years, finally our adoption is complete.

Below: At home. Our happy little boy with his beloved cuddly toys.

pounds, and the 0-3-month clothes we had sent out for him are definitely quite roomy. His skin is light coffee coloured, his hair very fine and black. His hands look so tiny, with his perfect little fingers curled tightly around one of mine. Those big, big brown eyes are resting now, hidden by his eyelids that flicker just slightly as he dreams. His ears are cute but certainly on the large side – Dom joked that perhaps they would aid him getting home – 'Perhaps he could flap home to us on his own without the aid of an aircraft, like the baby elephant Dumbo?'

It is not going to be easy for him, poor little chap, being moved to a new mother at such a tender age. Perhaps it is just as well our visit is to be a short one. That way, hopefully we will not unsettle him too much. Although we feel completely bonded to him in an instant, his bonding to us will take longer and will not be achieved in a few short days. This is for the best. Until we can return and have him with us for good, it is better that his bond continues with Ilana, his foster mother and certainly his 'mother' for the time being.

15 November 2007: Day two of our first visit to José

At two o'clock this morning I fell in love. As I held José in my arms and he fed from a bottle, he stared long and hard into my eyes; it felt like he was staring right into my very soul. I gazed into those deep, deep dark brown eyes. His eyes locked with mine and I felt we were suspended for infinity. His gaze was so deep, so trusting. I fell in love. I knew then that it would all be all right. He is our son and I love him unquestionably and totally.

I feel bowled over. My feelings of love towards him are so intense at this moment. I feel fit to burst. I quite simply could not love a biological child any more than I love José. So, this is what it is all about; this is what it feels like to be a mother.

Poor little José; poor little boy; No wonder he had been crying, screaming so much. He is teething and also has bad nappy rash. Imagine, your first two really painful challenges – first teeth

115

beginning to break through, and a raw, red bottom – and you are wrenched away from the only person you have known almost all your little life; wrenched away from the one who has been feeding, holding, cuddling and caring for you for the last five months of your life. You are suddenly abandoned and left with two strangers. No wonder he is scared and upset.

Last night as we walked around the hotel, bumping into other parents also trying to soothe their little ones, we felt a little calmer, a little less at sea. We were not the only ones struggling with unsettled babies. There is an amazing and bizarre kinship between all these adoptive couples, pacing the corridors of the hotel with their babies. The usual 'What's your name? Where do you come from?' and 'What do you do?' are replaced with only two questions – the only two questions that we all ask each other: 'How old is he (or in most cases "she")?' and 'What stage are you at?' (i.e. in the adoption process).

16 November 2007: Day three of our first visit to José

A second night has passed without incident – save for the odd screaming match or two. We feel a little more in control, and José certainly seems a little calmer.

When he is really upset, we take him on to the little balcony of our hotel room. Rocking him in my – or Dom's – arms and singing 'Edelweiss' or 'Truly Scrumptious' – yes, I was brought up on a diet of musicals – seems the only way to calm him. The fresh air seems to soothe him. Actually, the air is anything but fresh – Guatemala City has the most polluted air of any city I have ever experienced – but the breeze at least, and perhaps the rumble of the Chicken Buses as they go by beneath our window and the roar of the planes overhead (we are just behind the airport), seem to do the trick.

Dom has been doing a wonderful job on duty as chief bottle chef, sterilising and preparing José's feeds to ensure we always have at least two spare bottles in the fridge ready at any time of day or night.

I am in charge of nappy changing and washing and we take it in turns to play with him and hold him when he cries (well, screams – Ilana was right, he does not cry, and he certainly does scream). We slipped into these roles without discussion and make a good team – how on earth does anyone do this on their own, and even more staggering, how do they manage when they have other children as well to care for? For the first time I realise what a difficult task single mothers have. I take my hat off to them.

We feed him every two hours, night and day. I am sure that this is more often than most babies are fed at five months, but he only seems to want to take two or three ounces of formula milk at a time, so I suppose he needs to be fed this regularly. Certainly, now is not the time to change his routine.

Today he seems more settled and happier. I think he is beginning to get used to us. He really is an absolute little poppet. We spent ages lying on the bed together yesterday. I was lying on my front beside him as he lay on his back staring up at me, exploring my mouth and nose with great interest with his hands. It was so sweet.

He has these frantic exercise sessions every few hours, when he will lie on his back for ten or fifteen minutes at a time, punching the air with his arms as he moves them energetically up and down with swift, forceful movement, whilst at the same time frantically kicking his little legs. We reckon he is in training to be a boxer or a footballer, and currently hedging his bets by training for both. Earlier Dom joined in too, lying on the bed beside him, and I videoed them kicking and flapping their arms together. It looked very sweet and will be part of the video we are putting together for José so that when he is older he can see our first visit to meet him.

I cannot imagine having to hand José back to his foster mother later this afternoon. He is our son; we feel that totally and absolutely. We love him so very, very much already. We will just have to be brave and focus on the thought that the sooner we say goodbye, the sooner we will say hello again, and next time it will be for good. At the back of our mind, though, is the uncertainty of the political situation regarding adoptions from this country. Surely they will not

117

stop us bringing him home. Please God, they cannot do that.

Our attorney, Pedro, hopes that our case will enter PGN today. If everything goes our way, if we do not have a *previo* (a 'kick-out' over some discrepancy with the paperwork, which would mean a delay whilst it was sorted out and our case re-submitted), we could be through PGN in a few weeks. Dare I say we could even have José home by the end of January? Ever the optimist. Fingers crossed.

17 November 2007: Day four of our first visit to José

We depart today, flying back to the UK, back without our baby.

Our parting yesterday was absolutely desperate. Handing José back to Ilana was just about the hardest thing Dom and I have ever had to do. We both feel so completely bonded to our beautiful little boy, that to have to part so quickly and after so short a period together seems so, so cruel.

On top of this we had rather an alarming incident with him just before we had to hand him over, and felt even more protective towards our little son.

We had arranged with Ana, our agent's representative and translator, to meet her and Ilana in the lobby of the hotel at 3.30 p.m. José had his monthly appointment with the paediatrician an hour later and we were keen to be there too. We had frequently been warned that it is not safe for white couples to be seen on the streets with Guatemalan babies, so it was planned that Dom and I would travel to the clinic in one taxi, whilst the foster mother and translator would take José in a separate car. We would all then meet at the clinic for his appointment.

At 4 p.m. Ilana still had not appeared at our hotel. Ana was getting flustered. Our appointment was for 4.30 p.m. and it was important we did not miss it. Her brother was waiting outside in his jeep, but she was not keen for us to leave together. 'It is the police, you see,' she said. 'We don't have José's papers, they are with Ilana, and if the police stop us and see a white couple with a Guatemalan baby and no papers, José will be taken from you.' Reports of child-trafficking incidents in the papers have engendered a distrustful feeling by many Guatemalans towards westerners who are adopting children, and they accuse them of stealing or buying children to take them home to be sold as future wives for other family members or for their body parts. These rumours are ludicrous and totally unfounded, but the myth persists. Furthermore, the somewhat notorious Guatemalan police, who are always outside the front of the hotel, have been known to try and seize Guatemalan babies from white couples and demand payment for their return.

Ana's reluctant solution was that her brother, whose jeep had darkened windows, would drive us from the back door of the hotel, where the police do not hang around, to the clinic's underground car park. There was therefore no reason that anyone should see us leave the hotel or arrive at the clinic. Ilana would meet us at the clinic and take José from us after our appointment.

I asked whether Ana could take José herself in her brother's car and leave us to travel separately in a taxi. Surely that would be a safer option. She would not agree to do this as legally she was not allowed to be alone with our child. Until the adoption was completed José had to always be in the presence of either the foster mother or us, his future adoptive parents.

We therefore agreed with her plan – there did not seem to be much option – but it was perhaps against our better judgement.

Ana instructed me to sit in the back of the vehicle holding José, so that I would not be visible from the front. Dom was to sit in the front. As we drove away, this sudden feeling of fear came over me. *What were we doing?* Why had we not just said 'No'? Surely the appointment could be rearranged for another time? Was it really safe? Were we taking a risk? What if the police did stop us? They could take José, as we did not have his papers. Ana had seemed to think it was okay and we had been swept along with her suggestion. Now I was full of doubt and seriously full of fear. I could see the sweat dribbling down the back of Dom's neck as he sat in front of me. He later told me that at exactly the same moment he was

119

thinking exactly the same thoughts as I was and almost told the driver to turn around and return to the hotel.

We reached the first set of traffic lights, and suddenly someone was knocking sharply on the driver's window. I jumped out of my skin. So did Dom. José slept on peacefully in my arms. It was just a guy on a moped asking for directions, but I have never been so terrified. Fearing it might have been the police, I was almost out of the back door of the car and running down the street with our baby clasped tightly to my bosom. Just what sort of system is it when one has to fear the police so much?

As it was, the journey actually passed without further incident, and we reached the clinic without being stopped. Perhaps Ana was right and the darkened car was safe enough. I will never be sure. All I know is that that journey scared the living daylights out of both Dom and me.

The parting was totally devastating; so quick, so poignant, so, so desperate. After our appointment with the doctor, we descended into the bowels of the earth, or so it seemed: a dark, smelly underground car park. Dom was carrying José and I was following, trying to keep a check on my emotions, desperately trying not to cry. We reached the car and Ana turned to us and said in a kind tone, 'It is time now, I'm afraid. Ilana will take José now and my brother will drive her to her home.' Dom kissed José and handed him to me. I could see he did not want to let go of his son. I held José tight. I looked into his eyes and he returned my gaze, unaware of the poignancy of the moment. I kissed him one more time, whispered that we would be back for him soon, and then handed him to Ilana. I honestly do not think I have ever had to do anything so hard.

Dom and I had completely bonded to our beloved son during the last three days; José was just beginning to get used to us and now we were having to hand him back; hand him back without knowing when we would return, what the Guatemalan Congress would decide in the meantime regarding the possible suspension of adoptions from the country, or if we could indeed ever take him home.

Part of me – a very big part of me – just wanted to keep hold of him and run. Take him away. Find a way that did not involve this parting. I knew it was unrealistic. We had to go through the proper legal channels. I had to hand him back, but God, how hard that was.

We managed to control our emotions in the car back to the hotel but sobbed on each other's shoulders as soon as we reached our room. Our little boy ... oh my God, how we missed our little boy already.

A conversation that Dom had had earlier, and that he relayed to me over dinner that evening, played on my mind all night. The waiting room at the clinic was tiny and as I sat on a chair together with a group of Guatemalan women and their children, waiting for our turn to see the doctor, Dom stood in the corridor outside talking to Ana. She apparently grabbed Dom by the arm and emphatically said, 'Thank you. Thank you. Thank you. Thank you so much for adopting a little boy.' Dom was quite taken aback by this and told her she had no need to thank him; we wanted a little boy. 'But you see,' Ana replied, 'no one wants the little boys. Everyone comes to Guatemala and adopts little girls. You see the woman sitting next to Alex? She is one of our foster mothers as well. She is caring for four little boys at the moment. We cannot find families for them. Your attorney, Pedro, is at the moment paying for their care out of his own pocket, hoping that he will find families for them, but we just don't know. Otherwise what future will they have? They will probably end up like so many others on the street.'

I cannot imagine why no one else wants to adopt little boys. We are so happy that we are adopting José. He is the perfect little son for us, the son we have always dreamed of. And yet, it is true. Most adoptive couples seem to want little girls. When we were at the Marriott, there must have been twenty or thirty children there on visit trips with their adoptive parents. Of those children only one other child that we saw was a little boy. All the rest were little girls. I don't know why this is so, but I can see why Ana was so pleased we were adopting a little boy.

That evening we decided we would try and adopt another little boy, a brother for José. Until this moment we had thought we would return for a little girl, so that we could have one of each, so to speak, but not now. It was the boys who needed homes most. It would be fun for José to have a brother, but most importantly it would be giving a future to another child, a child who otherwise could well end up on the streets of the city. If the politics of the country allow it, we will return and adopt a second son. I hope we have the opportunity to keep to this resolution.

Those poor little unwanted boys. Not our José, though – he is the lucky one. He could not be wanted more. If only we had the means to adopt three, four or five of them ... okay, so maybe I am getting carried away ... but I just find this situation so incomprehensible, so tragic.

13

The Black Hole: Living in Limbo

21 November 2007: In PGN for five days

We arrived home on Sunday and are still reeling from the emotions of our visit. Our trip to Guatemala was wonderful and heartbreaking in equal measure: wonderful to meet our son at last, but so very heartbreaking to have to leave him behind and return to England without him. José is everything that we could have wished for; everything and so much more; the perfect little boy; our son.

I cannot believe how much I miss him. It is like a physical hurt, an ache right in the centre of my chest. I think about him all the time, wondering if he is eating or playing, sleeping or crying. It is a comfort to know that he is being looked after by such a caring woman, but we are his parents, he should be with us. Our visit made it all so real. We now feel that we *really* are his parents. His place is with us and it is agony that we are so far apart.

Our case entered PGN last Friday. Once the officials there have approved the adoption paperwork, they will draw up the adoption decree and our case can exit PGN. Maria, José's birth mother, will then need to give a final consent on the *Protocolo* (final adoption deed), after which the paperwork will be sent to the British embassy in Guatemala and the DCSF in England for their approval. Once we have received all these approvals, a new birth certificate, passport and visa can be issued and we can return to Guatemala to bring José home.

PGN is often referred to as 'the black hole', and with good

reason. Once your case enters PGN, it could take five to eight weeks to go through if you are lucky, or you could be unlucky and it could take six months or even more. It is impossible to say. You can get a *previo* (or 'kick-out') if you are missing any documents or for the flimsiest of other reasons – for example, a signature that they consider illegible or one that is placed slightly outside a signature box, or a document that has been stamped in the wrong place – and you then have to correct the error or problem and re-enter the process.

We hold our breath. Already it appears that we may receive a *previo* due to a problem with Dom's birth certificate. Although he is British, he was born in Malaysia and therefore his birth certificate is written in Malay. Only as our case entered PGN did Pedro, our attorney, realise this and that it therefore requires a notarised translation. Needless to say, we had not realised this would be a problem, or we would have alerted him to the fact months ago. It is frustrating, to say the least, that he has only noticed this problem at this late stage, when he has had our paperwork for four months.

More administration and a very complicated route are involved to get the necessary paperwork rectified. Dom's birth certificate is now being officially translated by a certified translator in Las Vegas. It will then have to be sent by courier to a notary to be notarised, then to Los Angeles to be legalised at the Guatemalan embassy, then to our adoption agency in South Carolina for an accompanying statement, before being couriered to our attorney in Guatemala for Pedro to translate into Spanish. He then will have to notarise his translation and put another accompanying statement to it and take both translations, as well as legalisations and accompanying statements, to PGN to add it to our dossier. (The dossier contains all our other documents which have already been translated by him into Spanish.) This will take a couple of weeks, by which time we may already have been kicked out of PGN because of this problem, and all because our agency and attorney did not check our dossier thoroughly enough in the first place. It is frustrating. Very, very frustrating.

3 December 2007: In PGN for two weeks and three days

We have now been back from Guatemala for two and a half weeks. Our case has also been in PGN for the same length of time.

This is without doubt the worst part of the process so far – this interminable waiting without a definite end in sight. At least with the other stages, we always knew, give or take a few weeks, when the next stage would take place, but with PGN there is no definite end in sight. Unless we receive a *previo*, we will be given no report about how our case is progressing, until we are informed, 'You are out' (i.e. our adoption case is approved). How we long to hear those three magical little words. We hope to be out by the end of January; we ache for that moment. The current estimate is that PGN should take about eight weeks, but we just do not know. I recently heard of one case taking eight months to be approved by PGN, and of another taking just one day.

We are finding it so hard since we returned. We had expected that the actual saying goodbye to José – after we had met and looked after him for three days – would be hard, but we had no idea how desperately difficult it would be to carry on life as normal after we had returned home. We think of him all the time. I look at his photographs a million times a day; carry them from room to room with me. Ridiculous, I suppose, but it is the closest I can get to him. There is one particular photograph that I find impossible to put down. It was taken just a couple of hours before we handed him back to Ilana. He looks so little and so very vulnerable, it just turns my heart over every time I see it. I can hardly bear to look at him, yet at the same time I cannot tear my eyes away.

José is *so beautiful*. Never has there been born a child so beautiful. Okay, maybe I am a tad biased in his favour, but everyone we show the photographs to agrees that he is a real little stunner. I feel it is perfectly acceptable for me to agree with their comments on his beauty – after all, I can take no credit regarding his looks. Indeed, Dom and I often comment that he is way more beautiful than anything we ourselves could ever have created!

I had no idea my love for him would be so intense after such a short time together. We miss him so.

4 December 2007: In PGN for two weeks and four days

We seem to ricochet from one crisis to the next as far as the political situation regarding Guatemalan adoptions is concerned. Today there was a further blow – this time dealt by the British authorities.

The DCSF have emailed me a statement which was issued today by Kevin Brennan, the Parliamentary Under-Secretary of State for Children, Young People and Families. It announces the suspension of adoptions of Guatemalan children by UK residents *with immediate effect*, in response to concerns – 'new evidence' – about the adoption process in Guatemala.

The statement is confusing. It states that with regard to *prospective* adopters from the UK currently in the process of adopting from Guatemala, the suspension will take effect at the point when the Certificate of Eligibility (CoE) was sent to Guatemala by the DCSF. The CoE is issued as a result of passing panel and in our case was issued back in June and arrived in Guatemala in July (2007). We should therefore be able to proceed with our adoption of José, but – and it is a big but – the final sentence of the statement is misleading. It states: 'This is the last point in the application process administered by the DCSF' – but that is not the case. After one's case exits PGN, the DCSF has to be contacted for its approval, in order that the child's passport and visa can be issued. So, do we have a problem or not? Can we continue with our adoption of José or not?

I immediately call the adoption department at our local authority and also, with some effort, I finally get through to the DCSF. Our local authority is not sure and the DCSF says that its *understanding* of the statement is that as our CoE is already in Guatemala and we have already been matched with a child, we will be allowed to proceed. However, it is emphasised that this is merely the department's *understanding* of the statement. The person I speak to cannot guarantee we will be allowed to bring our son home. They are not sure, they say. What do they mean, not sure? Not sure if we can proceed? Not sure if we can bring our little boy home? If the government has *concerns* over the adoption process, will it allow us to proceed?

If we cannot proceed and bring José home to the UK, then we will have to move abroad – but we do not want to live anywhere else. We want our families and friends around us as we bring up José. But we cannot abandon our son. Surely it will not have to come to that; surely we will not have to move to another country to have José with us – or will we?

There has been a flurry of emails on the various adoption sites all day. There is much discussion about the implications for those 'in process' and about the possible action that we can take. The general consensus is that first we need to request the government's evidence for taking the drastic step of suspending all adoptions from Guatemala before we can consider taking any action in protest. A letter is being written to demand this 'evidence'. We just have to be patient.

Be patient? How is that possible when we don't know whether we will be able to bring our little boy home? Just how much more patience have we got? How much more stress do we have to go through? How much more will be thrown at us before this journey is completed?

I feel physically sick. I feel like I have just done twenty rounds with Mike Tyson; like I am a punchbag or like I have been run down by a truck, a truck that keeps coming back for another go. As Dom said this morning when I rang him with the latest news, 'Just how much more of this can we take?' Not much more, I fear, but on the other hand, what option do we have? We will *never* give up in our quest to bring José home.

5 December 2007: In PGN for two weeks and five days

It appears that this statement from the British government about suspending adoptions from Guatemala by UK residents may well be a tragic knee-jerk reaction to the situation in Guatemala and be based on a lot of unfounded evidence. The statement has been issued over concerns that birth mothers are being paid for their children; that they are being coerced into giving up their young and that many of these children are being trafficked. This just is not the case. José's birth mother – like all birth mothers of children being adopted by UK residents – had to undergo very, very strict interviews with both the British embassy and the Family Courts in Guatemala to ensure that she had *not* been paid for her child; that she had *not* been encouraged to give up her child, and that the child was indeed hers to relinquish. Maria has signed three relinquishment documents confirming that she is not able to keep José with her and that she wishes for him to be adopted. She will sign a fourth relinquishment document when our case exits PGN. At any stage she is able to change her mind. In addition, her DNA was matched with José's under extremely secure conditions. Our case is not unique; every case has to go through the same extremely careful process if one is to bring a child from Guatemala to the UK. So why suspend adoptions carried out under such rigorous conditions from a country that has so many children in need of an adoptive home?

7 December 2007: In PGN for three weeks

We have received a letter from the DCSF confirming that, *as far as the British authorities are concerned*, our particular case will be allowed to proceed. One can only presume that they are confident our case is entirely legal, and that having progressed to such a stage they should not prevent it being completed. Whatever the reason, the British government's suspension of adoptions from Guatemala to Britain will not affect our adoption of José. Thank you God. A weight has been lifted from our shoulders, but we are almost too weary with the stress we are under to celebrate, particularly as we still await news from Guatemala as to whether the Ortega Bill will prevent our adoption taking in place in Guatemala. If the worst happens and the Guatemalan Congress does not agree to grandfather through the cases in process, then this good news from the DCSF will mean nothing.

We have been lucky that the DCSF will allow our case to proceed, but what about the other couples out there, as well as the single adopters, who were on the verge of sending out their Certificates of Eligibility, on the verge of being matched with a child? Their hopes are now dashed. This does seem rather harsh, to say the least, when there was no warning of this suspension. In Ireland they gave several months' notice, ensuring at least that couples would not start the process and be caught in the middle of it. Surely that would have been a fairer way in which to operate? Had we delayed our adoption process by a matter of a few short months, we would have been in that predicament too. There but for the grace of God ...

But most important of all, what will happen to all those children in need of a loving home in the future? It is so heartbreaking. Yes, more children will be living on the streets of Guatemala, abandoned at birth, aborted and so on. It may sound dramatic, but this is not an overreaction. This is the reality of the situation.

We want our adoption process to be absolutely scrupulous – as, I am sure, do all the other prospective adopters – which is why we spent so many months researching which country to adopt from and which agency we would use. We too are concerned about the issues being raised about corruption and malpractice. Over the weeks we may learn more and hopefully discover what 'new evidence' has led the government to make this decision to suspend adoptions from Guatemala into the UK. We have absolutely no doubt over the validity of our particular adoption case. We know that this is not a child-trafficking case and that neither malpractice nor corruption is at play, but I am not in a position to make a similar judgement on other cases. Perhaps there are other cases where other agencies and attorneys are less scrupulous. If that is the case, then yes, of course the corruption has to stop.

Meanwhile, we are still awaiting a firm statement from the Guatemalan Congress regarding the possible suspension of adoptions as of 1 January 2008 from Guatemala into the US, and we still do not know if and how this will affect adoptions from Guatemala to the UK – although this might now be irrelevant following the British government's recent suspension of such adoptions.

I have not written for a little while about the Guatemalan political situation regarding adoptions because, to be honest, I am quite simply *fed up* with the whole situation. Since September, when it first reared its ugly head, there have been statements, counter-statements, reports and denials posted on a regular basis on the various adoption websites. Often they directly contradict each other, presumably based on one or another person's interpretation of what is happening or on the translation of various reports from Spanish to English. Dates keep being issued on when the Guatemalan Congress will finally sit to discuss the Ortega Bill, and on whether it has now been passed for a second or third time (apparently although the Bill was passed for a first time in October, it is still necessary for it to go through this process before the Ortega Bill becomes law), and what clauses will be included. We remain hopeful that a grandfathering clause will be included to allow those children 'in process' to go to their new adoptive homes. We cannot contemplate the alternative and it is still uncertain as to whether it will apply to adoptions from Guatemala to the UK, or whether it will just affect those to the United States. It should not apply to the UK, as the UK is Hague compliant, but there is a general reluctance from anyone official to give us a guarantee. Our agency *thinks* our case will be allowed to proceed and our local council reckons we *should* be all right, but, understandably perhaps, no one is prepared to issue a statement confirming the situation either way.

The latest reports indicate that a new law will be discussed at an extraordinary meeting of the Guatemalan Congress on 11

December and that this law will replace the Ortega Law. And so the waiting goes on ...

11 December 2007: In PGN for three weeks and four days

A note someone has just posted on one of the adoption support and networking websites that we have joined strikes a chord. Like our case, hers is in PGN. She and her husband are currently on their visit trip and are about to say goodbye to their daughter and return to the US, not sure when they will be able to return to pick her up. She says:

> Our mindset must not be 'We'll miss you,' but instead, 'We'll be back be to pick you up soon.' Tomorrow we are one day closer to our PICK-UP TRIP! We must keep our eyes on our prize!

What a great attitude. She is right. Each day we are one day closer to returning to pick up José. We must focus on this; remain positive and keep our eyes on the prize – and what a prize he will be – instead of dwelling on whether politics will prevent us completing our adoption and on how much we miss him.

12 December 2007: In PGN for three weeks and five days

Yesterday the Guatemalan Congress approved a new adoption law (Bill 3735), which will come into effect on 1 January 2008. This law is supposed to ensure that adoptions meet with stricter requirements and it will enable Guatemala to meet with the requirements of the Hague Convention, an international agreement designed to protect children from trafficking. Adoptions will be taken out of the hands of agencies and lawyers and handed over to Guatemala's notoriously sluggish courts and the National Adoptions Council.

Unfortunately this law is so restrictive it is difficult to see how adoptions from Guatemala will be able to continue, and in the short term at least, it will still mean a suspension of adoptions from the country. Unbelievably, many people in Guatemala – including politicians – believe children are adopted to be used for organ transplants, and this belief is thought to be behind many of the clauses in this new restrictive law.

There is virtually no domestic adoption within Guatemala and the law makes no provision for the care of abandoned and relinquished children, so, once again, it is the children of Guatemala who will suffer.

However, the good news is that the Guatemalan Congress has agreed to include a grandfathering clause in the new law. This will allow the completion of those cases currently in process, providing they are registered with the Central Authority within thirty days. Hopefully this will at least secure the futures of the (approximately) five thousand children – including José – who have already been relinquished by birth parents and who have adoptive homes to go to. This Central Authority does not yet exist, but we presume it will be set up immediately.

The petitions to and subsequent involvement of the DOS and UNICEF almost certainly played a part in highlighting these in-process cases.

Phew! An entirely inadequate emotion, but we are so exhausted by the months of suspension; the months of not knowing; that I cannot even think how to describe my feelings of relief. I am not even sure *how* I feel any longer. Thank you God. Surely nothing else can be put in our way now? Please.

13 December 2007: In PGN for three weeks and six days

Today is José's half birthday. Today he is six months old. We raise our glasses to him over dinner in front of the most recent photograph that we have been sent; a photograph taken just two days ago at his monthly medical check. He is smiling. It is the first time we have seen his smile, and he looks a real cheeky chappy.

Tomorrow our case will have been in PGN for four weeks. Some friends who we met on the preparation course have now been in this stage for ten and a half weeks and still they wait. We had been told the average wait was seven to eight weeks, unless you get a *previo* – so obviously we are concerned. We feel like we are suspended in mid-air; in limbo. Certainly we are in a very deep 'black hole'. It is so frustrating.

30 December 2007: In PGN for six weeks and two days

Christmas has been hard, so hard without our little chap home. We are missing José so badly and feel like there is a big part of us stuck waiting in Guatemala, waiting to come home. We are both frustrated and a bit ratty. We are coping but finding it hard; very hard.

Still, we must be positive. A new year is almost upon us and in a couple of days we can truly say, 'José will be home this year.' How good that sounds. Roll on 2008. Maybe we will be lucky and our case will exit PGN within the next week or so …

I feel more hopeful now. I *know* we will be approved by PGN soon – hopefully by the end of January, which means he should be home by early March; certainly in time for Easter.

7 January 2008: In PGN for seven weeks and three days

A new year, but not the start to the year that we want. Unbelievable news has just reached us. We are devastated; frustrated; angry. Words are inadequate to describe our feelings at the moment.

On Friday, 4 January it was announced that PGN has stopped processing the in-process adoption cases as a result of the new adoption law requiring the registration of cases with the Central Authority.

When the new adoption law was passed in Guatemala in December, the government agreed to see through all in-process cases to completion *providing* they were registered with the new Central Authority within thirty days – that is, by 11 February. The Central Authority was due to be set up within this time frame, but as yet it has not been set up, and hence it is impossible to register our case. So, Catch 22 – the PGN will not process our case because it is not registered, but we cannot register it because the registering body (the Central Authority) does not exist. Hence, believing that there is no way it will be set up in time to have registered all the in-process adoption cases within the next four days, PGN has stopped processing cases and our adoption case has ground to a halt.

There is no news on if or when the government will set up the Central Authority. There is a change in administration on 14 January (that is, the old president leaves and the new president is instated), and I really cannot imagine it is likely to be top of the agenda for the outgoing or the incoming regime, so ... no one knows ...

Since September, we feel like we have been running full pelt in front of a giant wave; a tsunami. If we are caught by the wave, then that is it: we cannot adopt and cannot bring José home. But if we keep running, and we run fast enough, we will remain ahead of the wave and might just, just possibly reach our goal before the wave breaks. We keep hitting obstacles as we run. Some are easier to jump than others. Today I feel we have hit a large, fifty-foot brick wall.

Yes, we are devastated and frustrated, but of course we cannot give up. How many times have I written that? We just have to hope this delay will not last. We will not give up on you, José, we will bring you home.

This news has not arrived at a good time either. Today would have been the third birthday of our first little baby. I suppose it is just as well that when we lost him, three and a half years ago when he was just a little bean in my tummy, we did not know that three and a half years later we would still be waiting to have a baby to care for.

I have been crying just about all weekend ... poor Dom. He is so angry that we have yet another problem in our battle to bring José home that he too has been close to tears. It is not a good time. Just how many more setbacks do we have to face? How many more hurdles? I know I have said before that this is a real roller coaster of a journey, but honestly, it is quite unbelievable ... Voyage of the Damned? Only the thought of our beloved José, our beautiful little baby, waiting in Guatemala for us, his parents, to bring him home keeps us going.

8 January 2008: In PGN for seven weeks and four days

We both feel close to breaking point. We cannot sleep; we are both very tetchy and Dom has an aching back, brought on, I am convinced, by the stress. This latest blow has hit us hard. It feels like the final straw and we are heartbroken. Almost the hardest part is seeing Dom, whom I love so much, so upset. He is normally so strong for me, but even he broke down last night and sobbed. I felt so powerless to help. I try to be strong for him, like he is for me when I cry (which is rather more often), but it is hard when neither of us knows what will happen or how long the wait will now be before we can bring our beloved son home. It really is a testament to the strength of our relationship that it is surviving all the strains this process is throwing at us.

It is ironic I suppose. The grandfathering clause which was supposed to protect us is now being used against us in a way that was not intended. Apparently, according to Natasha, our adoption agent who is herself an attorney, the clause itself is unconstitutional. She says that legally 'a law cannot change a process that was put into motion according to another, previous, law', and yet this is exactly what the Guatemalan authorities are doing.

14 January 2008: In PGN for eight weeks and three days

Talk about cutting it fine. The new National Council on Adoptions (CNA, or Consejo Nacional de Adopciones, also known as the

Central Authority) was sworn in on the evening of 11 January, just hours before the deadline by which it had to be installed, and the same day that the outgoing president left office. It has extended the deadline date by which the in-process cases have to be registered, to 11 February.

We just hope that our case, and the others stuck in PGN, can now be registered and that PGN will reopen and start processing cases once more so that we can proceed to completion.

We are feeling much more positive. This latest setback – PGN calling a halt on processing cases until they are registered with the new CNA – will be just that: a (further) delay, but we should soon be back on course. Our case will soon be out of PGN. I am sure of it. We have to remain positive. It is the only way.

22 January 2008: In PGN for nine weeks and four days

One week later: oh, for goodness' sake – we have just heard that Colom (the new President of Guatemala) has thrown out those appointed to the CNA and replaced them with his own appointments. This has caused huge controversy. There is talk of the CNA now being disbanded and the new adoption law scrapped and ... back to the drawing board.

We have been told there could be further delays. I cannot even begin to put into words how we feel. I think we are beyond registering emotion. I just feel numb and very, very tired.

25 January 2008: In PGN for ten weeks

Last night I had the weirdest dream. We had travelled out to Guatemala to pick up José and on arriving there found that he was already walking and talking, and was about eight years old. I tried to hold and carry him like a baby – after all, I had expected to find him still a baby – but found he was too heavy. He was not happy that it had taken me so long to get there and I can still remember the feelings of panic and tremendous guilt that I had let him down by arriving so late.

Dom meanwhile has dreamt on three separate occasions that we arrive in Guatemala only to be turned back and told we cannot adopt José.

Dear God, please do not let this wait go on much longer. I am not sure we can stand it.

30 January 2008: In PGN for ten weeks and five days

... and still we wait ...

This morning I received an email from Natasha saying there is a further delay in the registering of cases with Central Authority (CNA) due to the original members being replaced by the new president. The new CNA members have decided to issue new registration forms, so although our attorney has been filling in registration forms which the CNA had issued a couple of weeks ago for all his cases, he is now being told these forms are no good.

Furthermore, there is now apparently a Central Authority (CNA)/PGN power struggle taking place. Central Authority wants PGN to verify the information on the registration forms and PGN is saying that it is not their job to do so ... and so it goes on. It beggars belief.

I think I am going to scream ... Aaaaaaaaaaaaahhhhhhhhhhhhhhhhh ... I think they could probably hear that in Guatemala. I certainly hope so.

1 February 2008: In PGN for eleven weeks

Very, very, very fed up; very, very, very frustrated. Yesterday was our deadline date – in our minds, that is. All along we have hoped and expected that our case would be out of PGN by the end of January. Just how much longer will we have to wait?

Last week we received José's monthly medical update and a recent photograph from Natasha. It really tore at our heartstrings. He looks so much older; a real little boy – no longer a baby. I know he is still a baby, but the difference in this photograph from when we saw him just two and a half months ago is very marked. He is getting older. He should be with us. The longer the wait, the more he will have bonded with Ilana and the harder the transition to us will be.

Heavy sigh . . .

I have been trying to take my mind off the wait by preparing José's 'life book'. In our adoption preparation course, we were told about the importance of an adopted child having his or her own book which would tell the story of their early life. I have spent hours and hours planning and discussing with Dom 'José's Story', as I am calling it, and I am now beginning to put it together. I want to concentrate on his history and heritage, giving him all the information that we have on his birth family and his early life before he was with us, as well as showing our journey to adopt him. It will be in three parts. Part one will show Guatemala, with lots of pictures depicting how beautiful the country and the people are, but also showing the poverty. Part one will also give José's history, the information we have on his birth mother, his birth and his first year with his foster family. Part two will show England, the country which will be his new home. It will show pictures of the best Britain has to offer (lots of pictures again), and Dom and I eagerly awaiting his arrival. Part three will be about José's move to us, his new family; our journey home (a picture of the world showing the route we took plus photographs of the aeroplane and our arrival in England), and lots of photographs of his new family. The book will finish with his christening and readoption in England. I hope it will be something that he will be able to treasure in the future and that will help him understand the reasons for his adoption and the extent to which we wanted him and love him.

Dom has also been spending his evenings working on editing the videos that we took in Guatemala on our first trip and our visit trip, so that they will be future mementos for José, showing him his country of origin and our first few days together as a family. We will take further video footage on our pick-up trip, for José to see when he is older.

Hopefully 'José's Story' and the videos will help give José a better sense of his history and roots and the country that he came from, and will help explain the reasons for his adoption. He will be shown both from an early age so that he will know his background from as young as he is able to remember when he gets older.

We have just discovered that there are two Central Authority offices operating, and it is unclear which one will be determined to be the 'official' CNA. Attorneys have registered their cases with the one that was set up in mid-January and now another, set up by the new president, is operating and requiring re-registration. Attorneys are now registering their cases with both to ensure they are valid with whichever office becomes the official CNA – how banana republic is that? What a mess. PGN is, I suspect, throwing up its hands in horror, and perhaps this accounts for so much delay in cases being passed.

12 February 2008: In PGN for twelve weeks and four days

Good news at last: We have now been registered with the CNA. We understand that the adoption attorneys in Guatemala have been working night and day to get all the cases registered by the deadline date of 11 February. Apparently approximately three thousand cases have been registered. Our attorney made the deadline with all his cases, including ours. *Big sigh of relief.*

Will this mean that our case will be processed at last by PGN? I certainly hope so.

19 February 2008: In PGN for thirteen weeks and four days

We have decided that we cannot wait any longer to see our son again. We have booked another trip out to Guatemala to see José before Easter. We had expected to have him home by then and we feel unbelievably frustrated and disappointed. Almost fourteen weeks and *still* our case is in PGN.

I frequently tiptoe downstairs at five thirty or six o'clock in the morning to check my emails for news, and we leap on the phone every time it rings, hoping that this time it will be *the* call we have been waiting for: Natasha calling from America to say our case is out of PGN. The disappointment on Dom's face each time he answers the phone breaks my heart. We try not to sound despondent when it is, yet again, a family member or friend calling to see how we are coping, but it is hard and I am sure our frustrated, upset voices must be off-putting to even the greatest friend.

20 February 2008: In PGN for thirteen weeks and five days

Not again. Not another setback. I feel in despair.

I managed to get hold of the telephone number of an English-speaking official at PGN and thought I would call to get a progress update on our case. After all, we have been waiting almost fourteen weeks, when we had expected to wait just eight. It took nine attempts to get through and when I enquired about the progress of my file, the PGN official said it was not in her system. My blood ran cold. What does she mean, 'not in our system'? Are our papers lost? Mislaid? Not even in PGN? What is going on? We got cut off before I could question her further and I rang back, but the line went dead.

I have called Natasha at our adoption agency in America but there is no answer.

I have now rung PGN back a further eighteen times (no exaggeration). The telephone network in Guatemala is such that every time I get through the line immediately goes dead.

I am shaking all over. I feel frozen. I feel like I am going crazy. I feel so powerless to do anything. To even find out what is going on. This is torture. What is happening?

I have tried calling Natasha again. I got through eventually and her assistant told me we are not supposed to contact PGN. It is not advisable and it is in our contract that we should not do so. I cannot find where this is written in our contract and frankly I do not really care; we want, we *need* some news. Our agency is not advising us on the progress of our case. We are not allowed to contact our attorney, Pedro, direct – we have not even been allowed to have his contact details – and Natasha's assistant was more concerned about telling me off for ringing PGN than about taking note of my concerns that we may not even be in PGN.

This is so frustrating. We are paying our agency. We are paying our attorney. Surely they should be able to contact PGN and get a progress update? What is it they want from us? Money? A hundred pounds? A thousand? Ten thousand (not that we have that sort of loose cash simply hanging about)? Our house? The shirt off our backs? The way we feel just now, you can have it all; just name your price and get our case sorted so that we can bring our little boy home.

I steel myself to ring Dom at work, to tell him the latest news. I delay calling; I cannot face being the bearer of yet more bad news. I call him eventually. He goes very quiet. I know he is struggling with his emotions. I cannot stand this. What has happened to our case? When will we be able to bring our darling little boy home?

21 February 2008: In PGN for thirteen weeks and five days and now 'out' on a *previo*

Not a good day.

Overnight we received an email from Natasha saying that we have indeed just received a *previo* – that is, a 'kick-out' from PGN. This means there is some problem with our paperwork, so our case has been thrown out. We are not sure what the problem is, but Natasha is trying to find out. This will then have to be put right before we can re-enter PGN. In effect we are back to where we were in November, possibly worse off, as we will have to rectify whatever the problem is with our paperwork before we can even apply to have our case re-submitted to PGN.

When did we get the *previo*? We were told that usually if you get a *previo* you hear about it within the first few weeks of entering PGN. The longer you are in PGN the less likely you are to have one. Is it that we were kicked out in those early weeks and our attorney has just not checked and found out about it? We feel so powerless and out of control. Is he on the case? Is he being proactive? It seems too much of a coincidence that the day I finally get through to PGN and find out we are not in their system is the same day we have a *previo*.

Natasha has sent me an email saying that I am in violation of our contract for contacting PGN and that it can jeopardise our case. This is ridiculous. I was only asking for information. The telephone number is widely published, apparently, and lots of adoptive couples call for updates. How can this be jeopardising our case just to ask for information? If I had not contacted PGN would we know that we had been kicked out? How long would it have taken to find out? How long before our agency advised us?

Furthermore, I have checked our contract. We signed that we agreed not to try and contact the foster mother or any members of the birth family, but nowhere is it written that we are not allowed to contact PGN.

Dom was in tears at breakfast this morning. We both were. I really cannot bear it when he cries. It breaks my heart.

In addition, we heard today that José has to have an operation on his umbilical hernia. It will take place at the end of this month. We had previously been told that after his consultation appointment, the consultant's opinion would be discussed with us and it would be up to us, his parents, to ultimately make the decision about his operation. Again we have been cut out of the picture. The decision is made without any consultation with us. Not that we would have stood in the way of good sense and reason if this is what the consultant recommends, but we are his parents for goodness sake. Do we not even deserve to be consulted over this?

He is not even christened yet. It is really important to me that he will be christened before he has the operation. I will ask Natasha to ensure that this is arranged.

What would we do without our families and friends, and even those strangers on the adoption blog sites whom I have never met but who are so supportive? The messages we have received today – I emailed the sites for advice and reassurance regarding our *previo* yesterday evening – and the calls from our families are keeping us going. I had lunch today with Sarah (Puff), one of my greatest friends. She was in tears when I told her our latest news. I was touched but cannot bear the thought that I am now even reducing my friends to tears.

22 February 2008: Entered PGN fourteen weeks ago today

Dear God, give us the strength to bear this relentless catalogue of events that never seem to see us moving forward; these stumbling blocks and negative responses to our every effort.

Natasha says no, it is not possible to get José christened before his operation. Apparently in Guatemala you have to have the birth certificate, have to register the child with a church, have to have parental consent, have to attend classes with godparents, and so on. Our agent has not spoken to a priest, in spite of our request – she has just been told this by 'friends' in Guatemala. I really cannot believe that a priest would turn down this request, particularly under the circumstances. Obviously we can give assurances that we will be bringing him up a Catholic and will have him blessed again with a ceremony, with godparents present, when he is in the UK if he has already been christened, but in the meantime we really would feel happier to know he has had a baptism or at the very least a blessing from a priest before his operation.

I have gone onto one of the many adoption blog sites to see if anyone knows a friendly priest in Guatemala City who can help. We have already lost one baby before he could be baptised. I cannot even contemplate something happening to José, but if it did …

25 February 2008: Entered PGN fourteen weeks and three days ago

Goodness, this is a long, arduous journey. We will get there in the end, but at times it is difficult not to despair. It is incredible how difficult it is proving to bring home a little baby whom we simply wish to love and to give a future.

We received good news and bad news over the weekend.

The good news first: A woman who runs one of the Guatemalan adoption support groups has used her contacts to find a priest in Guatemala City who is willing to christen José within the next week before his operation. The kindness of strangers – I have never even met this woman. It means so much to us both and has been a little ray of sunshine over a difficult weekend. Providing our agency plays ball – as it will be up to them to liaise with the priest to make the arrangements, as we have not been allowed the contact details for where José is living – then this should be possible. Fingers crossed. We have asked those we wish to be godparents if they would accept this role for José. They all accepted and it was heartening to see how pleased they were. It lightened our day in an otherwise pretty bleak weekend. We now have four more good people to look out for him.

The bad news is not as bad as it could be, though frankly I despair of PGN's pettiness. Our attorney, Pedro, has discovered the reason for our *previo* from PGN. Somewhere in our dossier, the PGN officials have found Dom's name written with his two middle names swapped round. This was obviously an administrative error, an error made, perhaps, when our documents were translated from English to Spanish. Because his name has been written in a way that is not on the name affidavit, they have thrown our case out. The name affidavit I drew up had 122 possible versions of our names (can you believe that it is possible to find that many variations?), but I had not thought to muddle up Dom's middle names. Hence, because the name affidavit does not tally with this entry in the dossier, we are thrown out.

It is unbelievable how petty bureaucracy can be. I think it is wicked; wicked that for such a ridiculously small reason they throw out a case and a little boy has to wait several more weeks, maybe months, before he can go to his new home. During this time he will bond more to his foster mother, listen to and learn a little Spanish, and it will just make it harder for him to leave his foster mother and move to us, his new parents. Not to mention the fact that we are missing so many of his milestones – his first word, sitting up for the first time; maybe even his first steps – missing all that completely unnecessarily, simply because of some clearly administrative – typing or translation – error, because someone at some stage has muddled up the order of two of Dom's names

Perhaps we should send in the SAS to airlift our little lad out. Frankly, it seems like a good idea at the moment.

26 February 2008: Entered PGN fourteen weeks and four days ago

Again I feel like I am struggling; struggling to cope. Dom is away on business in Spain and it is harder than ever to deal with this latest upset without him here.

I spent all yesterday going through every single piece of documentation we have ever sent our agency and attorney to check on the spellings of our names. I wrote a new name affidavit with our names in every possible, conceivable correct and muddled way that they could be written – and then duplicated the list in capitals as well. We now have 351 different ways of saying our names. This will have to be sent to Guatemala to be given to the PGN officials when our dossier is re-submitted.

I then sat at my desk and wept bitter, bitter tears. I really sometimes just wonder how much more of this I can take. Suppose they come across our names spelled incorrectly in another place in our dossier or find another reason not to approve our paperwork? Could we be thrown out again?

My asthma has returned; no doubt brought on by stress. I really am struggling, and not only for air. I feel like I am just going through the motions ... getting up; getting dressed; cleaning my teeth ... and all the time feeling so frail, so shaken up, so cold. Emotional upset is so draining, so tiring. I feel like I have been mown down by a truck or stuck on the fast cycle in a tumble dryer.

This kick-out of PGN may be due to an error which is relatively easy to solve – annoying, causing a further delay, but relatively easy to solve. However, in many ways it just feels like the final straw. I am not sure how much more of these upsets we can cope with. Dear God. Please.

Furthermore, Natasha has been in touch to say that it probably will not be possible to christen José even though we have found a priest willing to do so, because, first, we are not his legal parents yet and only legal parent(s) can give permission, and second, there are security concerns. That is, any excursion like this would expose José's situation and could result in someone becoming aware of it and reporting it to the police. Regarding her first concern, it is a difficult one. José is sort of 'between parents' from an official point of view. His birth mother has already signed three relinquishment documents, but the adoption has not been finalised.

Regarding her second point of concern, we have to bow to Pedro's knowledge of what is and is not safe. Our agent mentions that if, for example, a church employee or a parishioner were to pass on anything to the authorities, it could result in José being taken out of our foster mother's custody and we may not see him again. It seems incredible that even a christening is exposing him to peril – what dreadful dangers are there in Guatemala if a child cannot be christened for fear of his 'situation' – that is, the fact that he is being adopted – being revealed? We are not doing anything illegal here, but unfortunately there are those in Guatemalan officialdom (including many in the police force) who look for any excuse to prevent adoptions taking place. Obviously our attorney must do what he feels is appropriate and safe; José's safety is our primary concern and if a christening is not possible, then *c'est la vie*.

This is a low point, another low point, but I will bounce back. I always do.

28 February 2008: Entered PGN fourteen weeks and six days ago

I am feeling a little calmer today. Yesterday I was able at last to do something proactive in moving forward our adoption case. Dom and I signed our revised name affidavit in front of a notary and had the document notarised, and then I travelled into London to have it legalised at the Foreign Office (long and boring queue) and at the Guatemalan embassy (a lot of persuasion and fluttering of eyelashes required to get the document legalised the same day). I was even able to make it home in time to get the document sent out overnight by courier to Guatemala. So, all in all, a good day's work, and now at last the document is on its way to Guatemala. Once received, our attorney can have it translated into Spanish and then apply for our case to re-enter PGN.

I sent the various adoption support groups that we belong to emails warning other PAPs of the reason that we were kicked out of PGN so that they could ensure their name affidavits covered all possibilities. The supportive response has been unanimous: 'I don't believe it', 'How petty', and so on. One particular email I received was from a woman somewhere in America whose case has just exited PGN (successfully ... lucky her). She remarked that the PGN reviewer who kicked us out clearly was not aware that even though Princess Diana accidentally switched round the names of Prince Charles during their marriage vows, the priest did not discount their vows. That made me laugh.

We must look forward. We must not dwell on the (infuriating and petty) reasons for the *previo* from PGN and must instead look to the future and hope that we will soon be back in PGN and that this time they will not find fault with our paperwork and will process the case quickly. Please God.

Meanwhile, we are soon to travel out to Guatemala to see José again. I am feeling so excited at the prospect and it makes me feel less depressed over the latest setback in our case.

1 March 2008: Entered PGN fifteen weeks and one day ago

José had the operation on his umbilical hernia yesterday. It went fine and he is now recovering – big, big relief. Natasha emailed this news, also telling us that although he could not be christened, José was blessed by a priest before his operation. Great news.

Meanwhile, we have had our panel review in the UK. The panel decision confirming our eligibility to adopt is only valid for one year, and as our adoption is taking longer, we had to have this review. Fortunately this did not require another visit to the dreaded panel board. We simply had a short visit from a social worker – more questions – to confirm that our circumstances had not changed and to find out how we were progressing with our adoption. Quite a painless exercise when compared with everything else we are going through. Another box ticked.

In just ten days' time we will be seeing our little chap again. We cannot wait. Life is on the up. We just now need to hear our case is back in PGN and then at least we will be back to where we were in November ... and then hopefully we will start progressing forward again.

10 March 2008: Awaiting our second visit to José

We are back at the Guatemala City Marriott; back for another visit. This was supposed to be our pick-up trip, but with the latest PGN setback it is, again, just a visit. Still, better a visit than waiting several more weeks to see our little boy.

We have just had four days' holiday staying in a beautiful hotel on the beach in Puerto Morelos, near Cancún, in Mexico. It was meant to be four days of sunning ourselves on a beach, but the weather was ... how shall I put it? ... well, more Cornwall than Caribbean, but still, we have had four days' rest and relaxation, which certainly did us good after the emotional turmoil of the last few months.

We are so excited to see José again; a little nervous too, though not as nervous as last time. He will have grown so much, I expect, and we must prepare ourselves for the fact that he will have bonded that much more with Ilana, his foster mother, so the transition to staying with us will not be easy. I pray that we will be good parents and will not alarm him in any way over the next few days.

We have just spent an amusing couple of hours blowing up the toys – a rubber ring inside a material one with different animals and textures on it that he can sit in to play, and a sort of giant plastic sausage roll with bells in it that he can push along the floor if he is crawling. To save on space we have brought inflatable toys that could be flat-packed, but – only problem – we did not bring a pump, which I now see on the instructions is recommended. I am sure we made an amusing sight: a couple of asthmatics, purple in the face, on the verge of hernias, frantically blowing into these toys for all we were worth!

11 March 2008: Day one of our second visit to José

José arrived a couple of hours ago and is now having a morning nap, having cried himself to sleep. Poor little mite; he is obviously utterly bewildered by the new sights and sounds surrounding him. As he cried in my arms, he kept twisting his head this way and that, frantically looking over my shoulder for his foster mother. It was heartbreaking to witness. We can only hope that in the long term these visits are a benefit to him, helping him to get used to us so that once the actual transition – the permanent move from foster family to us, his forever family – takes place, we will be a little familiar to him and this will make his adjustment that little bit less painful. This is the purpose of our visits, but we are painfully aware that it is nowhere near enough and that our visits are far too infrequent: three days in November and now four days in March. I am sure that he cannot remember us from the last time we visited, but we just have to hope that there will be something slightly familiar about us. Dom and I had discussed this at length before our visit. I am wearing the same perfume and Dom has on the same aftershave that we wore last time, and in the meantime José has had the shawl I gave Ilana for him, onto which I had sprayed my perfume. We have brought some of the same toys and I am wearing the same jewellery. Even if he remembers nothing of us from the last trip, if we are lucky and do not have to wait too long before we return to pick him up for good, then perhaps he will remember us from this visit.

He is still little; very little. He is almost nine months old and yet the size 3-6-month Babygros that I bought for this visit are still very much the right size; a little roomy even. Guatemalans are small, though, and he certainly looks healthy, so I am sure we have no cause for concern. His tummy button is healing well after the operation a couple of weeks ago and we have been told he had the stitches out yesterday. We are pleased we delayed this visit from our originally planned date of the beginning of March, thus allowing him time to get over his operation in the familiar surroundings of his foster home, rather than with us, still very much strangers to him.

Apparently our case is now back in PGN, which is fantastic news. We just have to hope we will get no more *previos* and will be approved soon.

12 March 2008: Day two of our second visit to José

José is again having his morning nap, so I have a few minutes to write.

He has been with us for twenty-four hours now and there is certainly a difference between this visit and the last. It is noticeable how much more bonded he is to Ilana and how much distress the separation is causing him. His attitude to us has changed too. Last time – when he was five months old – he cried and screamed, and the only way to comfort and settle him was to hug him and carry him around soothing him. This time he is more actively rejecting us and more obviously missing his foster mother. He pushes us away when he is upset; arching his body away from us when in our arms, and on several occasions has only agreed to accept his bottle when lying in his cot rather than in our arms.

It is very difficult to witness his distress and hard to accept, but accept it we must, for it is not surprising he feels this way. Ilana has been his 'mother' for nine months now, and it is wonderful that he has bonded so well to her. Not for the first time, we are grateful we attended the adoption preparation classes in England. We have been taught that the more he has bonded to one particular carer – in this case, Ilana – the easier it will be for him to learn to bond to Dom and me in the future, and the more successful this bonding will be, though in the short term the initial transition will be harder. This obvious bonding to his foster mother and initial rejection of us is therefore a good sign, but it is still hard to witness.

Meanwhile we have had a meeting with Pedro, our attorney. With the aid of Ana as interpreter, he was able to respond to a few of our concerns and update us properly regarding our case. It appears that our case re-entered PGN on 22 February – just two days after we received our *previo*. In order to save time, whilst we sorted out the new name affidavit, Pedro re-entered our file with a legal document confirming the reason for the name discrepancy. It was a gamble doing it this way, but in order to save time, Pedro felt it was a gamble worth taking. We hope he is right. He is confident that our case

151

should be out of PGN very soon, maybe even this week or next. We have no idea how realistic his predictions are, but we feel a lot more optimistic after his visit. Certainly it will make handing José back to his foster family a lot more bearable if we know we are soon returning to pick him up for good.

13 March 2008: Day three of our second visit to José

José is nine months old today and has a little friend – his first friend, perhaps. There is a little baby girl staying in the hotel with her adoptive mother and elder brother and she has definitely caught his eye. She is called Maya and is eight months old. Coincidently, she was born in the same hospital as José, in Zacapa, some distance from Guatemala City in the east of the country, and José cannot take his eyes off her, and in particular off her mother, a lovely bubbly, chatty American from Ohio. Little Maya is playing it cool at the moment, but at breakfast this morning, she rewarded him with a smile which got José so excited that he flapped his little arms up and down, banging on the table with such ferocity that his bowl of cereal bounced onto the floor.

Maya's mother, Patricia, and I have decided to keep in touch. Maybe when José and Maya are older they can be pen pals. José might like a pen pal in America who originally came from the same part of Guatemala as himself.

We have been chatting to many of the other couples staying in the hotel with their adoptive children. Like the last time we visited, there were a number of adopting families – probably fifteen or twenty – staying at 'Baby Central', but the difference this time is that they are all – with the exception of ourselves – there on a pick-up trip rather than a visit trip. This difference compared with last time is indicative of the current situation, in which no new adoption cases are being arranged, and it is sad to see. With the exception of one couple, whose case has been in PGN for sixteen months, all the others entered PGN after us, and yet they are out now and here to pick up their children to take them to their new homes, whilst we will have to give José back to Ilana tomorrow and return home without him. We have often been told that there is no rhyme or reason as to the way PGN processes the cases, and this certainly seems to be the case. It is particularly harsh for us, but we have to accept it. Our time will come.

The hotel is preparing for the Easter festivities, as is the rest of Guatemala, with Holy Week commencing this Sunday. Easter, being the most important day in the Catholic calendar, is the largest festival of the year in Guatemala and is celebrated lavishly, particularly in Antigua, which has one of the biggest Easter celebrations anywhere in the world, second only to Seville in Spain. Churches throughout the country and the main streets of Antigua are strewn with brightly coloured, elaborately decorated carpets of flowers or sawdust. All morning in the hotel, artists have been carefully preparing an intricate design made up of three large pictures on the floor in the lobby. Measuring approximately twelve feet by four feet, this picture is made up of different-coloured sawdust and has taken the artists all day to prepare. The finished picture – carefully penned off with a miniature fence all around it – is quite astounding.

Dom and I have decided that one day we will return with José at this time of year so that he can take part in this most celebrated of feasts.

José is much more settled now. He is getting used to us and, I think, missing Ilana a little less. He smiles more, and when he is enjoying himself, frantically flaps his arms up and down and kicks his feet. He really is such a little poppet. I watch him as he sleeps, lying on his back with his arms outstretched, his eyelids flickering every so often even though he is oblivious to the world around him. He looks so peaceful and content and my heart goes out to him. Our son; our little miracle. I so want to find a way to help him with the transition from his foster family to our family and can only pray that he does not find it too difficult. Dom and I discuss this incessantly. Our feelings for him and our love for him have only strengthened in the months we have been apart. Already he feels a part of us, our darling son, our family, and it will break our hearts to have to hand him back to Ilana tomorrow afternoon.

José has a large number of mosquito bites on his arms and legs. This is not unusual in Guatemala, apparently, particularly at this time of year, but it has led to an amusing incident.

At breakfast, we got talking to another American couple with their baby and she noticed the red bite marks on his arms. 'Gee honey!' she said loudly and somewhat tactlessly to her husband, talking right across us. 'Take at look at that babe. What horrible marks on his arms.' I assured her that we were pretty sure they were simply mosquito bites. 'Does he have fleas?' she continued in a rather more abrupt tone. 'I gather a lot of these babies have fleas. *Ours* doesn't have fleas. No bites on her.'

We were seeing our interpreter and attorney a short while later and so I sought their reassurance, even though I was sure they were just mosquito bites. They both agreed that José, in common with a lot of children in Guatemala, had been bitten by mosquitos which were, in that part of Guatemala, entirely harmless.

A couple of hours later, Dom and I took José to sit by the pool and came across the same American women. '*Oh my gaad,*' she said in a voice loud enough to be heard across the country. 'Just look at that!' She was pointing to José and backing away as if we were lepers. 'It's all over his legs too. I don't want the measles. My baby doesn't want the measles.' I held José that little bit closer to me.

'It's OK,' I quickly replied, feeling very possessive and maternal towards the little boy in my arms. 'I have just checked and they are indeed mosquito bites. Nothing to worry about.'

'Walter!' she shrieked, across from one side of the pool to the other 'Wal-ter! It's OK. She's checked. The baby's not contagious. We're all right'. With that she nodded at us and walked away. Subtlety was obviously not her strong point.

Now every time we see them, Dom discreetly mimes the ringing of a large bell, whispering, 'Unclean ... Unclean.'

You could say we got our own back later that evening. Dom was using the microwave in the baby lounge at the hotel to sterilise José's bottles. He was using those very handy sterilising bags that are so brilliant for travelling. The same American lady was in the kitchen as well and asked Dom about the bags. 'They are to sterilise his bottles,' Dom said, showing her the bags. '*Sterilise?* You sterilise his bottles?' she asked. 'I don't sterilise my babe's bottles. No one told me to do that. Who told you to sterilise his bottles?' 'Just a paediatrician friend,' Dom replied, though that was not strictly the case. 'Oh,' he went on, 'but I *expect* your baby will be OK.' She left looking a little confused and concerned ...

Revenge is sweet – no one is going to insult our little boy and get away with it!

Maya's mother, Patricia, has been telling us a little about the current situation in Guatemala since the new adoption law came into effect two months ago. She speaks fluent Spanish and has just returned from having lunch with Pedro, who is acting as attorney for both her daughter and our son. Pedro's mother has been the foster mother for Maya, and so the two of them had invited her to lunch today before she departed with her new little daughter.

As we are aware, as of 1 January this year, only those adoptions in process are allowed to continue. No further children are currently being placed with adoptive families. Pedro told Patricia that, as predicted, this has seen disastrous results for the children of Guatemala. In just the last two months since January, one adoption official living in the capital has been approached by no fewer than sixty women unable to afford to care for their newborns and wanting to put them up for adoption. Poverty is the main reason they feel it necessary to relinquish their babies, but these officials are powerless to help. The women beseech the officials to take their children, fearing starvation for them, and when turned away, beg at least for a little formula milk or nappies – anything to give their children a greater chance of survival. The number of abandonments has sharply increased; indeed, just last weekend alone newborn twins were found abandoned in a shopping mall close to our hotel. I later read on the Toybox website that in the year 2008–2009, one child was abandoned in Guatemala City every four days; most were babies (www.toybox.org.uk, quoting from the Joint Council on International Children's Services, February 2009). Many of the babies are not found alive; those who are alive are taken to one of the few orphanages able to take them, but these are already bursting at the seams, struggling to cope with the crisis and the increased number of children being abandoned. The majority will join the population of street children if – and it is a big if – they survive at all.

Pedro has worked as an adoption attorney for nine years, and in that time, he reckons, he has placed approximately forty-five to fifty children a year with adoptive families overseas, but with the changes in the law, this will no longer happen – and this is just one attorney.

I find it hard not to weep at his reports. This would have been the future for all these children at the hotel, for José too, had they been born just six months later. Our children are the lucky ones; they will have families, food, clothing and an education. They will have a secure future. Many little ones, too many little ones, will not have the same chance.

Guatemala is a beautiful but in many places a dangerous country, particularly for children. There were 5,885 murders in the country in 2007 – an increase of 60 per cent since 2003 – at least 478 of which were of children. This year, in January alone, the number of children killed reached 80, and in February, a dozen bus drivers were murdered in the space of just two days in Guatemala City. The humanitarian organisation Caza Alianza recently reported that 70 per cent of Guatemalan children suffer some kind of physical or psychological mistreatment at home, in school or on the streets.

The soaring murder rates are largely due to the dramatic increase in organised crime, the weak justice system and ongoing impunity. Guatemala has the worst record for impunity in Latin America, with a single-digit conviction rate for murder. Many institutions, such as the police and the legal system, are so rife with corruption that they are seen by many to be not only involved in a large proportion of the killings, but often to be instrumental in them.

The Dutch ambassador recently described Guatemala as 'a paradise for organised crime', and the near-total absence of justice can be seen largely as a legacy of Guatemala's long civil war that ended twelve years ago, and which resulted in a long-standing cover-up of gross violations of human rights by the state, a weak, corrupt and ineffectual judiciary, and a profound lack of accountability on the part of society.

On 14 May 2007, in a BBC News report entitled 'Crime Dominates Guatemala Campaign', James Painter reported that Amnesty International had stated that:

> ... 'clandestine groups' are active in Guatemala. These groups consist of criminal networks involving 'the business sector, private security companies, common criminal, gang members and possibly ex and current members of the armed forces'.... In recent years, Guatemala's growing role as a transit point for large shipments of cocaine has given more economic clout to criminals. Another factor is the growth of the youth gangs, known as *Maras*. Some estimates put their membership higher than that of the 19,000-strong police force.

Even Guatemalans fear being out on the streets of the capital city, particularly as dusk approaches. The following tale is indicative of the fear of many. Patricia's foster mother visited Patricia and little Maya a couple of days ago. Midway through the afternoon, she suddenly got into a complete panic that she might not get home before it was dusk. Patricia offered to call and pay for a taxi for her, which she gratefully accepted, but she remained agitated as she was concerned that it wouldn't reach her home before it grew dark. She does not live far from the hotel but said that it was so dangerous in Guatemala City that on no account could a woman ever be out on the streets, even in a taxi, after dark.

What sort of a state of affairs is it when it is not safe at six o'clock in the evening for a woman to travel in a taxi from a smart hotel to her home? Indeed, six months after our return we met a couple who had stayed in the Guatemala City Marriott on their pick-up trip shortly after our stay. From their hotel window, in broad daylight, they witnessed a murder – a man shot and then bundled into the boot of a car – right outside the front of the hotel.

The situation here in Guatemala City is desperate. It is hard for us – from such a relatively safe country – to understand how difficult life must be for many people, in particular women and children, here. We moan about the 'yob culture', about our government and our health service, but really we have little cause for complaint. If we are sick, we can see a doctor. It may not be at a time most convenient to us; it may not be the doctor we want to see; but we have a free health service. In Guatemala, for the majority of people, if they get sick they either die or they get better, without medical help. Less than ten per cent of the population in the country ever get any medical help in their entire lives. They simply cannot afford it. We complain about the British government and our government services, but our police do not go around beating up and killing homeless children; our leaders may not always be completely honest, but the situation cannot compare with Guatemala, where extradition is being sought for three of Guatemala's last four presidents on charges of fraud. We complain about the lack of safety on our streets, but we can travel by taxi from a central London hotel to our homes at dusk without fear for our lives. When we compare the government and life in Britain to many other parts of the world, we can only be thankful.

14 March 2008: Day four of our second visit to José

We have a happy little bunny in our arms today; well, if not happy, content at least. José is really beginning to be much more at ease and I think a little happier in our presence. He still does not reach out for us when he is upset; he certainly has not bonded with us yet; but at least he is not unhappy in our presence. We know it will take time for him to bond with us – we will have to wait for our return next time to start that process – but there is certainly a marked difference in his mood now from three days ago when he was left with us.

José is certainly a character and will, I am sure, be quite the cheeky little monkey. He waits for us to be watching him before he throws his rattle from his high chair, so that he can see our reaction. Yesterday when Dom tried to catch it he immediately switched it to his other hand, waited until he had caught Dom's eye, and then dropped it from the other side, grinning all the while. He loves his food – good! He will fit in very nicely in our family! And he takes great delight in grabbing the spoon from Dom or me and smearing his food all over his face, eyes and hair: feeding time at the zoo indeed. He enjoys getting a reaction from us and is in every way acting like a real little boy. We can't wait to see his character develop further.

Ilana is doing such a wonderful job with him. It is clear how much he loves her and she him, and as difficult as the transition will be for José, I know it will break her heart to have to hand him over to us for good. Obviously she has known from the start that she will only have him with her for a while – it is her job – but it is clear that this particular child means a lot more to her than the other children she has fostered. Her husband, Carlos, came with her to pick José up from us. He speaks a little English and explained how much José loved Ilana and Ilana loved him. 'He is like a son to us,' he explained.

José was thrilled to see Ilana. He literally jumped for joy, flinging himself out of our arms into hers and kicking his little feet. It was both delightful and heart-warming and, at the same time, heart-breaking to see. We are so lucky. We could not have wished for better foster parents for him, for a better start in life for our little chap. They are looking after him so well and giving him so much love – the love he so richly deserves, as do all children – but at the same time it was quite hard to see just how readily he flung himself from us, without a backward glance. I should not expect more; of course he is pleased to see Ilana, and it really is great that he feels like this about her, but I would be lying if I said it did not hurt me just a little.

It is actually too hard to write further about handing José back to Ilana this afternoon. It tore our hearts yet again, but now we just have to focus on believing that our case will soon be out of PGN and that we will be returning to him before too long.

Next time, little boy; next time we will not be leaving; next time you will travel back with us and stay with us for ever.

At least this time we know that he will definitely be coming home. Last time we visited, in November, we had the worry about the change in the adoption law and whether the new law would prevent us from bringing him home. That was far, far worse. It will not be long … It will not be long … It will not be long. If I say that often enough, I will continue to believe it and hopefully the positive thoughts will make it happen.

17 March 2008

We arrived back yesterday, after quite possibly – actually, definitely – the worst journey of my life.

On our last night in Guatemala, having handed José back to Ilana, I awoke in the middle of the night with the most violent stomach cramps imaginable and … well, suffice it to say that I spent the rest of the night in the bathroom being very, very ill indeed. Something I had eaten had seriously disagreed with me.

The following morning I was so ill I could barely lift my head from the pillow, and had to force myself repeatedly to crawl to the bathroom. We were due to leave the hotel at 11 a.m. for our flight home from Guatemala City to London, with a change in New York, but I was obviously in no fit state to go anywhere. I have most certainly never felt so ill.

Dom went to speak to the hotel's duty manager and explain, in no uncertain terms, how they had obviously poisoned me. To give them their due, they immediately leapt into action. A doctor was called, apologies made, and the previous night's dinner deducted from our bill.

The doctor arrived within ten minutes of the hotel's call (not something I would even have expected in England). Instead of a Spanish-speaking doctor and perhaps a member of staff to translate, the door opened and in walked four medics, carrying a stretcher and oxygen canisters, together with a doctor and three members of the hotel staff! My god, what had Dom told them? It was like a scene from the television drama *ER*. In spite of feeling like death, all I could do was lie back in bed and giggle.

The doctor gave me some antibiotics, which he assured me would make me feel lousy, and painfully cramp my stomach, but it would at least get me home. Well, I made it home but it was not a journey I would like to repeat. I lay groaning on the floor at Guatemala City Airport before our flight – how undignified – and the flight attendant at the gate almost refused to let us board, so concerned was he about my state of health. I felt even worse on the long flight to New York and then on an equally tedious one to London, though in retrospect I suppose Dom pushing me at breakneck speed in a wheelchair through Newark Airport to try and catch our flight was quite amusing.

We were so late for the London flight because our flight from Guatemala City to New York had been delayed, and once we arrived in New York we still had to reclaim and check back in our luggage before catching our onward flight. Having done so, we realised it was already time for the flight to depart and we still had to find our departure gate, on the other side of the airport. As Dom charged across the terminal, pushing me in my wheelchair – I was too ill to walk – with me clinging on for dear life, our hand luggage in my lap, and trying not to throw up or fall out, he was panting so hard that I was terrified he was going to have a heart attack, and/or that the chair would hit a ramp and I would go flying out as Dom lay sprawled on the airport floor. We only caught the onward flight by the skin of our teeth, arriving as they were closing the doors – and what a sight we must have made, Dom dripping with sweat and panting like crazy; me a delicate shade of green, swaying as I stumbled onto the flight, doubled up with stomach cramps. No wonder the passenger seated next to us looked uncomfortable as we approached.

27 March 2008: Entered PGN eighteen weeks and six days ago

Every few days I hear news of another person whose case has exited PGN. Almost all of them seem to have entered the process after us. Surely, surely it must be our turn? I feel like we are living in limbo.

Apparently a lot of attorneys offer the PGN officials bribes to get their cases through quicker. Pedro told us that he was not the fastest of attorneys but is one of the few who refuses to engage in this practice. He is too ethical to do that, and whilst we were glad to hear of his moral stance when he told us, just at this moment I do rather feel that perhaps a box of chocolates? ... a bunch of flowers? ... a bottle of whisky or even a wedge of cash might just be in order. All we want is to get out of PGN so we can bring José home.

Meanwhile, we just have to hold on to the fact that our son is receiving the very best care possible. Of that we are certain. We received an email from Carlos, José's foster father yesterday. According to our adoption agency, we are not supposed to be in direct contact with our foster family, but when Carlos requested our email address so that he could keep in touch after José had moved to us, we could not see the harm in giving it to him. We had not expected to receive correspondence from him so soon, so it was with much surprise and delight that we received the following sweet little note from him just ten days after our return (translated into English by my brother-in-law, Mark):

> Good evening, may the Lord our God bless you. I greet you with much affection hoping that all is well. I tell you that José is very well, we took him to the swimming pool at the weekend, he loves the water, his skin turned a precious pink, I am very sorry that we forgot the camera and it pains us that we couldn't take photos, we

can't return as it is 80 km from our house. But we will take it next time and will send the photos through this way [I presume he means by email]. I am very sorry to write in Spanish but the mistakes in my writing embarrass me, I'll try next time. Goodbye, may God bless you with riches and abundance. Jose sends you a smile with two teeth.

How wonderful to have such delightful and personal news direct from José's foster family rather than simply the medical updates we receive from Natasha.

28 March 2008: Out of PGN! ... José is coming home!

Oh my God ... oh my God ... oh my God ... Thank you God, thank you God, *thank you God*.

We have just received the best possible news; the best news in the whole wide world; the best news we have ever had.

This morning – just an hour ago – I turned on my computer to find an email from our adoption agency sent late last night saying: 'José's case was approved by PGN today, Thursday.'

We are out of PGN! Eighteen weeks and six days after our case entered PGN, one day shy of five months, and, strangely, a year to the day since we passed adoption panel, we have been approved by PGN. Finally *our little boy is coming home!*

Cloud nine? I am on cloud nineteen; cloud ninety-nine; cloud nine hundred and ninety-nine even. I have never, ever felt so excited, so relieved, so thrilled.

I am shaking so much I can hardly type. I want to sing from the rooftops; announce to the world; celebrate, celebrate, celebrate. Off to buy a bottle of champagne. Cancel that – off to buy a case of champagne!

163

Part III
Coming Home (April–July 2008)

14

The Final Stretch:
Enough to Try the Patience of a Saint

2 April 2008

I feel slightly calmer now but still so very, very excited. We celebrated the news of our exit from PGN all weekend. We have been inundated with messages of congratulations from family, friends, colleagues and even friends of friends who we do not even know... even the champagne hangover feels good!

I have spent the last few days in a whirl. Too excited to do anything constructive and yet already planning José's homecoming, I am writing lists, lists and more lists of things that need to be done beforehand. There are a million and one last-minute arrangements to be made.

Practicalities: We have about four to six weeks to wait before we can collect José and bring him home from Guatemala. Although he is now officially our son in Guatemalan law, we need to await the entry paperwork to be able to bring him into the United Kingdom. First, the PGN documents confirming approval of our adoption have to be translated from Spanish to English and his new birth certificate has to be issued. The British embassy in Guatemala then has to review the documents to confirm approval of José's entry into the UK, after which the documents will then be sent to the DCSF in Britain for the DCSF also to review and approve his entry into this country. Meanwhile, José's passport has to be issued in Guatemala and then, once DCSF approval is received, the passport will be sent to the British embassy in New York for the visa stamp, then returned to Guatemala for us to collect. A lot of paperwork will be winging its way from Guatemala to the UK, from there back to Guatemala, then on to New York and back to Guatemala before we are allowed to bring José home.

Bureaucracy permitting, we should be able to bring José home by mid-May, a month before his first birthday. His first birthday was always our *absolute deadline date*. We originally wanted him home by last Christmas (unlikely but possible), by Easter (likely but did not happen), and then by his first birthday (essential).

Although we are obviously totally thrilled to be finally planning José's homecoming, the timing is not ideal from a business point of view. The May/June period is the busiest time of the year for conference and corporate event organisers. This is not a problem for me as I have not taken on any new business this year in anticipation of José's arrival, but it is awkward for Dom, who has spent the last couple of days trying to find a way to extricate himself from the many events he should be organising over that period so that we can travel out to Guatemala to bring José home. His two weeks' paternity leave may have to get postponed until July, but at the very least he needs enough time for us to spend a minimum of a week in Guatemala, letting José get used to us and begin to come to terms with losing his foster family, before making the big journey home.

We are itching to get on the next flight out to Guatemala to collect our little boy, but yet again we have to exercise a little patience whilst we wait for the bureaucratic wheels to slowly turn.

7 April 2008

We have bought presents for José's foster family – a leather wallet for Carlos, a gold cross and chain for Ilana, and a little hardback book of pictures of the UK for them both, to show them the country to which we will be taking their charge. They have been so good to José, we wish we could do more for them, and certainly money would be more useful, but we have been advised that the gifts we have chosen for them are appropriate presents to give, and we certainly do not want to insult them in any way.

We received another sweet email from Carlos again, translated as follows:

> ... José is very very healthy ... at each moment he makes us laugh. Now when we take him to church he starts to applaud when he hears the music or when we say to him bravo, I will show you in the photos. Please know that José is very well, is very intelligent, a blessing to you all. I pray to God that the day that you take him fills us with peace, knowing that we cannot have him but he will be with you, that you will love him and give him a better life. God bless you for what you are doing for José.

I cried when I read this. How lucky we are; how lucky José is. We could not have wished for a more perfect – more warm and loving – foster family for him for his first year of life. They have given José unconditional love and care at a critical time in his life and we will for ever be grateful to them. How hard it will be for them when he leaves, but as they say, they cannot have him for ever. It is good to hear that he is taking photographs of José for us (we had given him a small disposable camera on our last visit). We will keep in touch with them and in turn send them regular photographs and perhaps one day we can return on holiday with José and they can see him again.

José's passport has been issued: a Guatemalan passport in the name of José Bemrose. Dom was so excited to see that José now has our surname. Since the UK government does not accept the Guatemalan adoption process as a legal adoption in the UK, we will have to adopt José again in Britain, and he will then receive a British passport. Meanwhile, he can enter the country with his Guatemalan passport, providing it has the entry visa stamp. We still await the visa. Once we have it, we can bring him home.

11 April 2008

A reality check in the midst of our excitement – a sobering true tale that had us realising how lucky we are. You just never know what is round the corner in life. That much is for sure.

We met a lovely American couple when we were staying at the Guatemala City Marriott Hotel on our first visit trip back in November. They were adopting via the same agency as us and they were also on a visit trip, seeing their little daughter for the first time. She was three months old and was adorable. They were approved by PGN just a couple of weeks before us and this week were due to go back out to Guatemala to take her home.

Today I received an email from them saying that they were unable to bring their daughter home as planned. Once they got to Guatemala this week, they realised that she has some potentially very serious medical issues that had not been disclosed to them. As a result, the US embassy was not willing to issue her visa at this time. They have had to leave her with her foster mother and return without her and are trying to establish exactly what her condition is. They do not know what the outcome will be. It is shocking and very worrying that they seem to be getting absolutely no support or advice from Natasha. This is exactly where one's adoption agency is supposed to step in and help, but Natasha seems to want to wash her hands of the situation. Furthermore, apparently they came across another couple, also on their pick-up trip, who had not received the correct paperwork. The birth certificate and other vital documents were missing, and again, they received no assistance from Natasha.

My heart goes out to our American friends. I wept as I read their email. One cannot imagine their pain at having to return without their beloved little daughter. I will pray for them and will light a candle for their daughter in church this Sunday. I only wish I could do more.

15 April 2008

Just at this critical moment, we hear rumours that our adoption agency in America has gone bankrupt and that Natasha has had to take another full-time job. I am not sure if this rumour is true, but if it is, it does not come as a great surprise. With the new adoption law passed in Guatemala, intercountry adoptions from Guatemala will cease to exist, at least for the time being. We are one of the last cases to be allowed through, and as our adoption agency predominantly specialises in adoptions from Guatemala, their main source of business has dried up. Furthermore, it has been absolutely impossible to get through to our agency on the phone since February. I have been sending emails literally every couple of days since then asking Natasha to call us, but have received no replies to my emails and there is no answer when I telephone. What little response we have had to our emails has been much slower and less informative than previously. Whereas up to Christmas we were full of praise for the agency and entirely satisfied about the service we were receiving, since then we have had very poor or pretty much non-existent service.

We are so close to completion; so close to bringing José home. I cannot even begin to consider that anything could go wrong now. Natasha is meant to handle all the adoption arrangements until we literally have José back in this country. Many months ago we had to pay her in full for her services organising our adoption, but already we are being left to make the last-minute arrangements without her support. If we go out to Guatemala and find that vital documents – for example, a birth certificate or even the actual adoption deed – are missing, then we would not be able to bring José home.

We are confident that Pedro and our agent's representative in Guatemala are still doing a good job for us, but it is very worrying that with the 'adoption business' grinding to a halt, we could be left somewhat high and dry if we have a problem.

We are a little nervous, to put it mildly. I am weary of all the stress of trying to make these arrangements and just want to have our little boy safely home.

171

We will not rely on the increasingly less efficient service of our agency. We ourselves will try and ensure the remainder of the process runs smoothly and without any hitches. I do not care if this is against our adoption agency's contract. Natasha is failing to fulfil her side of the contract at this stage by disappearing and not responding to our queries, so why should we worry about upholding our side of the bargain?

I have spent much of the day on the phone to the DCSF trying to establish whether they have received the paperwork from Guatemala yet, and then to the British embassy in Guatemala to chase up the paperwork and find out when it will be sent to England. Only then will we feel we can decide on dates and book our flights. Even then it will be a bit of a gamble, guessing when the approvals will be received, and when the passport and visa will be ready for José to travel to England with us.

We are hoping Pedro will be able to arrange for us to meet Maria, José's birth mother. The ball is in her court; it is up to her to agree only if she wishes to meet us, but it would be wonderful – if a little nerve-racking – to meet her. If we do, though, we can perhaps find out a little more about her to tell José when he is older.

I have spent some time today trying to write a letter to Maria – a letter that we can hand her if we are able to meet her, and if not, a letter that hopefully Pedro will be able to give her. I will get it translated into Spanish and I am sure she will then be able to find someone to read it to her. It is a difficult and emotional task. I want to convey to her our immense gratitude that she gave José life and to assure her that we will always take good care of her/our son; that we love him as our own, and will try and ensure he grows up healthy and happy and secure in England, but also knowing about her and about his native country, Guatemala.

I have also prepared a little album of photographs for Maria of us, our families – José's new family – his new home, the neighbourhood and our local park. There are spaces for additional photos which I can send to her in the future if she wishes to keep in contact.

She may not want these things; she may not wish to meet us; it may be too difficult for her. However, if she does then it may help to reassure her about José's future, and perhaps give her some comfort about the no doubt very difficult decision she had to make in giving José up for adoption.

16 April 2008

It is very frustrating. The British embassy in Guatemala, whom I am in contact with on an almost daily basis at the moment, keep promising to fax over to the DCSF their approval of the entry paperwork, so that the DCSF can confirm its approval as well and José's visa can be issued, but nothing is happening. Today, someone from the British embassy says they are so busy they have no idea when they will be able to deal with it ... Aaaahhhh! It is enough to try the patience of a saint!

We are itching to book our flights, but with every stage taking so much longer than it was meant to, it is difficult to know when the necessary paperwork will be ready.

Once again, we are experiencing the endless frustration and stress of waiting for the next stage. Even this late in the game, things can go wrong, so we cannot relax. We are feeling stressed again and impatient; very impatient.

24 April 2008

It seemed to take forever to start happening, and now it is all happening at once. Within the last three days the British embassy in Guatemala and the DCSF have approved the entry paperwork, José's passport has been sent to the embassy in New York for the visa – why it has to go to New York to get the visa, I have no idea – and today I received an email saying the visa had been issued.

We have booked our flights. We depart on 5 May and José will be brought to us on 6 May. He will be in my arms on the sixth of May and we will become a family; a family for ever. At long last.

We have decided to spend a week with José in Guatemala to allow him time to get used to us before the long flight home. We will depart Guatemala on 13 May, fly back via Panama City and Madrid, and arrive in England on 14 May – home at last with our little boy. We are dreading the lengthy return journey – three separate flights – but to avoid having to apply for another visa for José (American or Mexican), it is necessary to fly this route. Travelling via Miami or New York or Mexico City would have been quicker and would have entailed only two flights, but would also have involved a day's queuing in Guatemala City to sort out the extra visa for him.

Oh my God, this is just too, too exciting. We have a date, a date when we will become a family at last and a date when we will arrive home. I am beside myself with excitement.

Dom is away on business again. His clients, rather sweetly, have officially voted José 'Cutest Baby on the Planet', having asked to see a photograph of him. They are right. He really is the cutest baby on the planet. *Our* cutest baby; *our baby.*

28 April 2008

This time next week we will be en route to Guatemala. Having waited for this moment for so long we are so excited, so very excited. I am nervous too. Nervous about whether I will be able to cope with a baby; very nervous about the long flight home; nervous about whether José will be able to cope with the transition from his foster mother to me; nervous about whether he will learn to love me; nervous about all the changes to his life, and to our lives too.

José's room has been ready for months, many months. His cot is made up; the baby changing table has nappies at the ready; there is a Babygro at the foot of his cot for the first night back; a pile of clothes is waiting to be packed; and there is another little pile for when we return. I have learnt and practised how to open and fold down the buggy.

The conservatory has been transformed into a playroom. The

wooden floor that splinters so badly is covered in a foam A-Z puzzle mat; his toys are neatly laid out (that will not last long); and the electrical sockets are covered by little child guards.

I spent the weekend preparing, cooking and freezing meals suitable for a baby. Thirty-two mini puréed meals are now neatly stacked in the freezer. I had long dreamt of the moment I would be preparing these meals and enjoyed every minute of their preparation. Bottles are sorted – some to take and a couple to remain behind – already sterilised for the moment we arrive home. I have even stuck the NHS Direct telephone number and a list of symptoms that indicate if a baby is suffering from meningitis (God forbid) to the inside of a cupboard in the kitchen.

Never has a mother been so prepared ... Quite nauseating really!

1 May 2008

Only four more days to go. Four more days until we fly out to Guatemala. Five days until we become a family.

Meanwhile, although I am incredibly excited, I am starting to get a little melancholy on behalf of José. Sad for the sorrow that is about to enter his life and the grief he is about to go through. He will be losing everything he is used to – language, sights, sounds, smells, textures, tastes – but most of all, he will be losing Ilana, his foster mother; the woman who has been his mother for the last eleven months; for as long as he can remember. One minute he will be with her, in a cosy, familiar environment, and the next he will be given to strangers – albeit his new parents – and will have to travel halfway across the world to a new home. I cannot get away from the thought that, to him, this will seem like a frightening kidnap. I do so hope that there is something familiar about us to him when we meet again. That he recognises the sight of us; our smell, or something about us from our last visit. This will, I hope, make it less frightening for him. He will be grieving. In time he will not remember Ilana; in time the loss of his birth mother will become more

175

important – wondering what she was like; why she had to give him up and so on – but in the short term it is the loss of his foster mother that will be so painful for him. We have no doubt, the first few weeks will be hard.

Such wrenches and losses – of his birth mother and then his foster mother – so early in life can psychologically harm a child if the situation is not handled sensitively. We have learnt from the preparation course we attended and the books we have read how damaging this can be. It is a disturbing process for one so young. Certainly he is gaining in the long term: a permanent mother and a father, a secure family environment, sufficient food and an education, not to mention the abundance of love he will have from us and from his extended family. He will never want for love. Of that we have no doubt.

However, there will always be a little piece of the puzzle missing for him, a lack of information about those early days of his life, fuller details about his birth family and a true understanding of his heritage and native country. We will teach him about Guatemala, about his birth family and heritage, and we will ensure that he goes to Spanish classes to learn the language of his native country and will maintain links and friendships with other families who have adopted from Guatemala so that he can have Guatemalan friends. We just have to hope that by these efforts, together with our support, our understanding and our love, we can reduce the size of this missing piece of puzzle.

It is important that right from the start he is taught who he is and where he is from; that the story of his birth and adoption is not shrouded in mystery and that there is never any shame attached. Adoption is a wonderful thing and it is important that it is perceived as such. We will celebrate what happened so that he learns it is a good thing; a positive thing. Not a negative. José will not always *be* adopted; he *was* adopted, and now he is our son. He is our family. In the future we will refer to the process not as 'You are adopted', but as 'You were adopted'. I think the difference is important.

I feel so blessed. Motherhood is one hell of a responsibility, the greatest responsibility any woman can have, and all I can say is that I am going to do everything possible to give this little bundle of joy the future he deserves.

Meanwhile, thank goodness our case is out of PGN. I heard today that PGN has again closed. It has put a 'temporary hold' on all the final in-process cases it is dealing with whilst it awaits an audit. There is talk of the CNA interviewing the birth mothers for a second time to ensure they have voluntarily relinquished their babies, even though the poor women have already been interviewed at length on this very point by the Family Court and by the embassies. It also wants to look into cases that appear to have exited PGN too quickly in the past. What are they going to do about that now? They surely cannot call back cases that are already out, children who have already gone to their future homes in different countries, can they?

Once again I say that we will be very relieved when we have our little boy home.

15

Into Our Arms for Ever

6 May 2008: 'Family Day'

The day has passed in a whirl. José's foster family – Ilana, her husband Carlos, and two of their three teenage children – brought him to our hotel early in the morning, together with Ana, our agent's representative and interpreter. It was a desperately sad moment for them and a moving one for us. They played with him for a while whilst we questioned Ilana again on his schedule, his likes and his dislikes, what cheered him up when he was upset and what his favourite games were.

The moment came for them to say goodbye. We had assured them we would keep in regular contact and would send photographs as he grew, but after eleven months of looking after, caring and loving him, this was never going to be easy. They were all in tears. Sensing the mood, José started crying, and even Dom and I were fighting back the tears. As they left the room, Carlos kept repeating, 'Please rock him to sleep ... please rock him to sleep ... you must rock him ... please ... please.' Even as I now write these words, tears spring to my eyes as I recall the moment of their parting. It was such a hard moment for them and consequently a bittersweet moment for us.

Poor José was distraught to see them go. He screamed and screamed. For a while we felt powerless to find a way to comfort him, but eventually he cried himself into an uneasy nap, sobbing as he slept. It was heartbreaking to witness. All we wanted to do was hug, kiss and comfort him; all he wanted was Ilana and the family he knew and loved. Poor little mite; he had no idea what was going on.

Our visit to the British embassy – to collect his passport and visa (the final stage in the adoption process in Guatemala) – was, after all this time, something of an anti-climax. After so many months – years even – to get to this point, I think that I expected ... I'm not sure what ... not a fanfare exactly, but certainly something more than an impersonal visit to a window in the office to sign a couple of pieces of paperwork, after which we were handed his passport and visa and our other paperwork. Five minutes was all it took and we were out on the street, a couple no longer ... for evermore, a family.

What a wonderful feeling, to be holding our child in my arms and to know that, this time, it is for always. We will celebrate this date – 6 May – for the rest of our lives. I don't think the British have a name for the day an adopted child is given his new parents, but we will not be naming it 'Gotcha Day' as the Americans do ... a term that rather makes me shudder. We will name it 'Family Day' – the day we at last became a family.

6–12 May 2008

Our first week as a family – how good it feels to write those words – was spent in the town of Antigua, staying at a delightful *posada* (bed-and-breakfast villa) run by a friendly retired American couple who many years ago had adopted a little girl from Guatemala, and who now live in Antigua, renting out their three spare bedrooms to adopting couples only. The posada was idyllic, a real oasis in the busy town, with all the rooms leading onto a beautiful palm-filled shady courtyard with swinging bench-chairs, overlooking a lawn and a little swimming pool.

The time was so very precious to us; our first week together as a family, but it was difficult, very difficult – in particular the first three days. We really struggled and even considered changing our flights to bring José home early, not sure that we could cope with such a desperately unhappy baby on our own in a foreign country, trying to find suitable food for him to eat and ways to comfort him.

Our poor little boy was grieving for his foster family. He was understandably frightened and desperately unhappy to find that they were no longer there to care for him. It was heartbreaking to witness his distress and be so powerless to help. We were happy and unhappy – happy, ecstatically so, that we had our son with us at last; but unhappy that we were finding it so difficult to cope and were unable to comfort him. I wasn't sleeping – in fact I went for three days with literally not even five minutes' sleep I was so wound up – and this just made matters worse. Furthermore, the heat was sapping from us what little energy we had left. It was the rainy season but the rains had not yet arrived and instead the pressure and temperature were building, as they do before a big storm. (The weather only finally broke as we drove to the airport to go home.)

Then suddenly, on the fourth day after José came to us, as he lay on our bed, he kicked his little legs, flapped his arms and gave us a big smile. It was the moment we had waited for. I knew we had turned a corner. It was going to be okay. José was going to be okay with us. In time he would bond with us, but for the moment, his smile was all we wanted.

Hours later he suddenly stood up on unsteady legs, grabbed my hands, and set off round the patio for his first few shaky steps. It was an exciting, moving moment. Here we were, a family at last, with a baby who was beginning to accept us, and here was this momentous moment in any child's life – his first few steps – and they were to be witnessed by us. (Ilana has told me he was already standing holding on to furniture, but he was not yet walking.)

In retrospect, we were glad we persevered and remained in Guatemala for these precious first few days together. It was important for José to begin to get used to us and start to come to terms with his loss before the trauma of the long flight to a new home in a new country. By the time we left, he was calm and, if not totally happy, he certainly seemed content in our presence.

13 May 2008

On the final day of our trip we got the call we had been anticipating; wanting, and yet at the same time dreading. Maria, José's birth mother, had agreed to see us before we left with him for England, his new home. Way back in the summer, at the time when we accepted the referral to become José's parents, we advised our agency and attorney that, should the possibility arise, we would definitely like to meet José's birth mother and if possible maintain contact with her. We feel it is important that we should keep this door open for José's sake so that if in the future he wishes to meet her, we will have done everything we can to maintain contact.

At the same time, if not actually dreading it, we were concerned about meeting his birth mother. Suppose she told us things we would rather not know? Suppose she did not turn out to be the woman we had imagined – wanted even – as a birth mother for our son? Might we regret making contact?

We were aware too that this meeting was asking a lot of Maria. Apart from the emotional trauma of once again meeting the child she had had to relinquish for adoption, giving up a child for adoption is not acceptable in many Guatemalan communities and if it becomes known that a woman has relinquished her baby, it can place her in extreme danger. Tragically, there are a number of cases of birth mothers who have been killed for being in contact with adopters, so extreme caution had to be exercised. We therefore left the ball in her court. If she felt she wished to maintain contact and/ or meet us, then it would be arranged. If not, then so be it. The decision was with her.

We were advised before our arrival that she had agreed to meet us, but on the day in question she did not show and we presumed that she had changed her mind, perhaps taking fright at the prospect; maybe she decided it would be too traumatic for her, or perhaps she felt it would endanger her family or community if her actions were discovered.

However, on the day we were due to leave Guatemala, as we were literally packing our bags, we received a phone call from our attorney. Maria had just turned up in his office in Guatemala City. She had walked and travelled by bus from her village and wanted to see us, and José one last time, before we left for England. We finished our packing in haste, and en route to the airport made a detour to our attorney's office to meet her. We were again reminded of the dangers of Guatemala City. Our driver, recommended to us for 'secure armed transfers', felt it necessary to remove his watch and gold bracelet before taking us into the city. On the short walk from the car park to our attorney's office – literally less than twenty paces – he insisted on walking behind us to ensure our safety and assured us that he would wait by the entrance to escort us back to his car after our meeting.

It was an emotional, heart-rending meeting. Maria looked so young; so fragile; so vulnerable. She cried to see the son she had given birth to but had felt unable to keep, and we so, so felt for her situation. With the aid of Ana, who acted as our interpreter, we reassured her that we would give José all the love and care we could possibly offer; we would feed him, educate him and keep him safe. These were some of the primary concerns she had voiced when interviewed regarding her decision to give him up for adoption. She knew this was the best chance for her son, but it did not make it any easier for her. We also assured her that we would tell him about her, his birth mother, saying only good things and explaining her situation, and that we would bring him up to know his roots and his native country of Guatemala.

She was able to give us more information regarding her family and circumstances – all vital information that we shall treasure and remember to pass on to José – but most important, we now felt we knew a little more about her and could, hand on heart, tell José in the future of this woman who loved him and wanted him but who at the same time loved him enough to want to ensure that he had a future; a future she felt unable to give him.

She agreed to pose for a photograph with us and José so that we could give it to him when he is older. Finally we gave her a letter we had previously written and an album of photographs of him and his future family and home, and then we left.

It was an emotional meeting but we have no doubt that seeing Maria had been the right thing to do. In particular, we were very pleased to have been able to take a photograph of her, together with José and us. With so many negative articles in the press about child-trafficking it will be reassuring for José, I am sure, that he will actually have a photograph of himself and us with his birth mother, thus proving her agreement to the adoption. We can only hope that it will be possible to maintain contact in the future.

16

Home at Last

14 May 2008

I will treasure the memories of our arrival in England for ever. As our plane touched down at Heathrow Airport, I could not stop the tears welling in my eyes. At long last we were home with our son; it was the culmination of a two-year, seven-month-long journey involving extensive research, interviews, battles with bureaucracy and government authorities and four trips to Guatemala to adopt a son. So long-awaited and longed for, and at times so elusive and seemingly impossible to achieve, it had finally happened: we were arriving home with our son; a family at last.

A momentous day for José too: today, at the age of eleven months and one day, he has arrived in the country that will be his new home.

As the immigration official checked José's passport, visa and documentation, Dom and I held our breath. There was a pause (an eternity) and then, with a smile, he said, 'Congratulations. Your son may enter England.' Six little words but they meant so much. Dom and I looked at each other and beamed. It was only then that I realised how tense I had been, still concerned that something could go wrong, that a piece of paperwork would be missing or incorrect. I felt a weight lift from my shoulders as I relaxed. We had made it; we were home; well and truly home with our son.

Our families had turned out to greet us and to welcome José. Dom's parents, my mother and my two sisters were waiting in the arrivals hall at Heathrow with big grins on their faces, a bottle of bubbly and a large 'Welcome Home José' banner held aloft. Cheers greeted us as José took his first few steps on English soil, holding tightly on to both my hands. There was hardly a dry eye in the house. Our arrival and this greeting from our families – sharing in our joy – was quite simply the happiest moment of my life.

July 2008

We have been home almost two months now and both baby and parents are settling in to their new routines and lifestyles.

The first few days back home poor José suffered a little setback. Hardly surprising, considering all the changes he had recently experienced. It was probably the new surroundings and climate, not to mention the jet lag (there is a seven-hour time difference between Guatemala and England), that caused him to revert to the way he had been during his first few days with us. He was unsettled and unhappy, crying a lot, but this time he was clinging to us – a good sign that he was beginning to bond.

After three days he was starting to settle and was becoming more playful and smiley.

By mid-June, when we celebrated José's first birthday, he had become the happy, lively little boy his foster family had often described. He was settling in remarkably well. He is a bright, bonny boy, with an engaging smile; full of joy and energy. He babbles away continuously, and kicks his feet and flaps his arms when he is having fun. He protests energetically and vocally whenever he is made to lie down, whether it be for nappy changing or for a nap. He loves dogs, teddy bears, being pushed on a swing and playing in the bath. Most importantly, he has survived the transition and is happy again. He is learning to bond with us, his new parents, and we are learning to be parents. He is a normal little boy, experiencing all the love, attention and fun that children deserve. We feel so blessed and so very lucky.

José is very attached to a little monkey that he holds tightly in his arms whenever he sleeps. When we first accepted the referral for him to become our son, we sent a bag of clothes and a couple of toys out for him via another family travelling out to Guatemala (it is virtually impossible to courier out packages directly as they almost always become impounded in customs and never reach their destination). One of the items we sent out was a little monkey for him to cuddle. We bought two at the time, keeping one so that when he returned with us to England he would have the identical toy – something familiar – to cuddle. It worked and he loves his monkey – George – and never sleeps without it.

Having spent more than twenty-five years working and the last twelve of those years running my own company organising corporate events and conferences, it is an extraordinary feeling to be at home all day bashing bricks together, singing nursery rhymes, mixing formula milk and changing nappies, but I can honestly that I am loving every minute of it. Yes, even the wake-up calls at 2 a.m., the dirty nappies and the screaming fits. They are a part of motherhood and I have waited so long that I am basking in every moment of it. It feels like a dream; I can hardly believe this is me, *a mother at last.*

The first few times I took him out in the buggy, I felt like I was play-acting or in a film. Could this really be for real? Am I really a mother? I almost expected someone to leap out of the bushes shouting, 'Cut. Take a break.' I think I am doing all right in my new role, although we did have an amusing incident three days after our arrival home. José developed a rash around his neck, and in a panic I rushed to the surgery to see our doctor. As she took off one layer after another to examine him, she remarked that he did seem to be wearing rather a lot of clothes. 'He was born in Guatemala and has only just arrived here,' I replied. 'It is a much hotter climate and I am concerned he doesn't get a chill in this cold weather.' Her verdict? A heat rash. In my paranoia that José would suffer pneumonia in this colder climate, I had put on so many layers that the poor little mite had come out in a heat rash!

Dom too is getting used to his new role and relishing being a dad at last. As I expected, he is already showing signs of being a great father; kind, gentle and loving, but also fun and humorous. Having always wanted a son, Dom has lost no time in starting as he means to go on. José already has England rugby pyjamas (white with the red stripe and red rose), a whoopee cushion and a miniature remote-control helicopter. I am sure it will not be long before he has been signed up for the junior Harlequins rugby team and our sitting room has been taken over by a train set.

Our families fell in love with José from the first moment they saw him. My mother would have moved in given half the chance, and delights in every moment she can spend with her new grandson. A child at heart, she has a natural understanding of children that wins them over every time. José adores her and has such fun whenever they are together. Dom's parents, too, clearly adore him and are eager to visit and help out whenever they can. José's cousins fight over whose turn it is to hold his hand and whose turn to push him on the swing. They all embraced him from the start and he immediately became an important part of the whole extended family. We are incredibly lucky to have such a supportive family, who have been there both during our journey to adopt and also now that we are home with our son.

Meanwhile, thank God we were approved by PGN when we were. It is apparently still not approving any more cases until all the birth mothers have been re-interviewed. Recalling birth mothers at this stage must be a logistical nightmare – many of them have no fixed address, and in some cases it is simply not possible to find them.

Meanwhile, according to a report by one of the attorneys handling adoptions, birth mothers are being offered money to cancel their pending adoptions – a payment of 500 quetzals (approximately forty pounds) per month until the child turns eighteen years of age. Considering the government does not apparently even have enough money to take care of the children currently entering orphanages, how on earth does it plan to fund these promises? I gather the view of most attorneys is that it is unlikely the money will ever be forthcoming.

Part IV
The Final Hurdle
(July 2008–March 2009)

17

Readoption in the UK

23 December 2008: Seven and half months after we returned home with José

Two days before Christmas – seven and a half months after José has returned home with us – and at 8.30 in the evening the phone rings. 'Hello, it is Celia Jones here. I am José's guardian. I'm just calling to confirm I have arranged a solicitor for José and we are seeking legal aid. I think we should arrange a meeting.' What? Trying to remain polite but feeling my hackles already rising by her rather assertive tone, I reply, 'Sorry, but I'm not sure who you are or what you are talking about.'

This was not strictly true. I was aware that José was going to have a 'guardian' appointed by Cafcass (Children and Family Court Advisory and Support Service) whilst we went through the adoption process in the UK, but I did not expect a call at that time in the evening, so close to Christmas, and her tone was, to say the least, rather domineering. I was not going to make it easy. I wanted more of an explanation from her.

To clarify, the British government does not accept the Guatemalan adoption process as a legal adoption in this country, and hence we are in the process of adopting – or readopting, as it is commonly referred to by those who have already legally adopted their children overseas – José in this country. José entered the country with a Guatemalan passport and an entry visa which allows him to remain in this country for up to two years. In order for the visa to have been submitted, the British embassy in Guatemala and the DCSF in the UK had to be confident that the Guatemalan adoption paperwork was in order and that it was a legal adoption in Guatemala. However, before this two-year period is up we will need to have adopted José in Britain, after which he will become a British citizen and will be given a British – or rather an EU – passport. Quite what happens if the readoption takes longer than two years, or if for any reason the courts here do not agree to legalise our adoption, I do not know. I mean, they can hardly send him back to Guatemala, can they? Frankly, it would be over our dead bodies.

The court elects a children's guardian to act independently from the family and the social workers to ensure the child's best interests are met. This guardian has legal responsibility for the child until the adoption is finalised and therefore needs to visit us, check our care and, like the social worker, write a report to be presented to the judge. If José required an operation during this period, it would be the guardian's responsibility to sign the consent form and not us. The guardian has quite a level of power in the proceedings. It is for the guardian to evaluate what is in a child's best interests and the judge places considerable weight on his or her opinion. I had to calm down and be polite.

I was taken aback by this 'Christmas' phone call because I had not expected the guardian to be elected until the first court hearing in January, though perhaps I had misunderstood the timing. But a solicitor? Legal aid? What was she talking about?

'Er, thank you for calling to introduce yourself,' I added, trying to sound a little more friendly, 'but I don't really understand what you mean about a solicitor and applying for legal aid. We have actually already hired a solicitor to handle the readoption.' 'That is a solicitor to represent you and your husband in the adoption case,' she retorted. 'As José's guardian I do need to ensure that *his* best interests are met and therefore he will require his own solicitor.'

What? Our little boy, aged eighteen months, requires a solicitor because the British social service system cannot trust that we, his parents, have his best interests at heart? I thought I had heard it all during the last three-plus years, but once again I am surprised by the system. Without any possible reason for doubting us and our care for José, Cafcass have hired a solicitor for our son and applied for legal aid, which presumably the tax payer will have to pay for, to ensure that we, his parents – who love him more than anything in the world, who would lie down and die for him, who could never conceive of doing anything to harm him – are serving his best interests.

I know I have to accept this. I appreciate the fact that the guardian is part of the system and it is probably right that someone independent should check the details of the adoption and that we are the best solution in terms of his care. It is the system and we have no alternative. We have had far worse thrown at us in the last three years, but it was her tone that I found so offensive. By the time I put the phone down, I was spitting mad.

6 January 2009

This morning I went to the Principal Registry of the Family Division, a court in High Holborn, London, for the first hearing of our case to legally adopt José in Britain.

Last November, six months after José came into our care, we were able, or rather a solicitor acting on our behalf (yes, involving more costs) was able, to apply to court to adopt José in Britain. Now, two months on, there is an initial court hearing for the formal application, at which point the social worker's report is given to the judge. The guardian then writes and submits her report to the court and a second court hearing will be held, at which point, hopefully, the adoption will be confirmed.

Today was the first hearing. Present on one side of the court room, in addition to myself, was our social worker Katrina and our solicitor. On the other side were José's 'guardian' and *his* solicitor. Not used to court settings, I rather felt like I was on a film set. Neither Dom nor José was present as it was only necessary for one of us to attend the first hearing, so Dom was at work as usual and my mother was minding José.

Although I had taken an instant dislike to Celia when she rang just before Christmas, I found my first impressions were entirely unjustified. Meeting her today, I found her to be perfectly charming, sensible and very likeable indeed. I must eat my initial words.

While I was aware that we had to go through the adoption process in the UK, I couldn't help but feel rather taken aback when I heard our solicitor announce to the judge the reason for the hearing: 'José Armando is currently *residing* with Dominic and Alexandra Bemrose and they wish to apply to adopt him.' As far as we are concerned, we *have* adopted José; he is our child, our son, not just some child currently *residing* with us. To us, our family and friends, the legal adoption in Guatemala confirmed that José was our son, and this UK readoption process is merely a formality, a legality. However, this is not strictly the case. Although we have adopted José legally in Guatemala, as our social worker put it to me, he is actually currently in 'legal limbo' in England until we have adopted him through the UK adoption system as well. Such is the adoption process and once again we have to go through each stage of it.

Our social worker handed over her report (the Annex A/Rule 29) to the judge, who would take it away and read it, along with all the adoption paperwork confirming our legal adoption of José in Guatemala. The judge scheduled the second hearing for 25 February, at which point, hopefully, an Adoption Order would be confirmed and José would then be our legal son in this country as well as in Guatemala. The judge would then set a date to meet all three of us for a more informal meeting and then our adoption of José would finally be complete and we would be able to apply for his EU passport.

Our social worker Katrina's report was written on the basis of the nine visits she has made to us since José's arrival in May, the Guatemalan adoption paperwork and her re-interviews of our referees. Nine visits in eight months – an unnecessarily excessive number to our mind. Every few weeks, she has visited to check up on the care we are giving José, how he is settling in and how we are coping. As with the earlier home-study process, it is an intrusion and not altogether a welcome one, but as with everything else on this 'journey' it is a part of the process and we just have to accept it; in theory at least; in practice, her visits have left me demented. Perhaps it is just that I have had my fill of intrusive questioning from social workers, but unlike the social worker who prepared our home study, I have found Katrina so pessimistic in her responses. Her retort to almost every positive reply I make regarding José's progress is the negative 'At the moment . . .', with a heavy emphasis on the 'At'.

For example, Katrina: 'Is he sleeping okay?' Me: 'Yes, fine. Usually sleeps all through the night.' Katrina: 'At the moment . . .'

Or, Katrina: 'Does he seem to have bonded all right with you and Dom?' Me: 'Yes, definitely.' Katrina: 'At the moment. There's a long way to go yet you know. A lot can still go wrong.'

Can she not just accept that this is not one of her *problem* cases, and that we are not going to require ongoing attention from social services? Can she not simply share in our joy at a successful adoption?

In addition, the friends and family members who provided references for us for our initial home-study procedure have had to be re-interviewed and we have again had to have numerous checks and medicals done, not to mention the piles of paperwork we have had to submit.

Once again it has seemed a never-ending process, but the difference has been that this time José is with us, so we are more relaxed. Surely the court will confirm our adoption? They can hardly send him back now, can they? How would they do it? Where would they send him? Back to Guatemala with a tag round his neck like Paddington Bear? He would have nowhere to go. The whole process does seem a total waste of time — for the social workers and for us — and of money, seeing as we have already legally adopted him in Guatemala. A pointless exercise.

Dom has suggested that once the readoption is completed and we no longer have to have social worker visits, we amend the 'No circulars and no junk mail' notice on our letterbox to read 'No circulars, no junk mail and most definitely no social workers'. I am inclined to agree.

12 January 2009

Oh dear. I have just had a disagreement with Katrina, our social worker, surely failing the unspoken Rule Number 1 of adoptions: *Never fall out with your social worker.*

She arrived about thirty seconds after José had tripped and fallen in the hall, banging his head on the bottom step of our wooden staircase. He was not badly hurt but screaming blue murder and within seconds, in spite of my quick application of arnica cream, he had a bump the size of an egg. I opened the door to Katrina with José still screaming in my arms, and explained what had just happened. I was dismayed and upset at her immediate response: 'Does he fall often? How many accidents *exactly* has he had since his arrival?'

Maybe I was just being oversensitive, seeing as she is a social worker, but her tone and the questions that immediately sprang from her lips did seem rather accusatory. If she was trying to imply that this was anything other than the usual stumble and the resulting bump and bruise all children have when they are learning to walk ... 'Don't you dare go there' was on the tip of my tongue, though I just stopped myself in time from saying this out loud. Nevertheless, I could feel tears smarting and my blood starting to boil.

As she handed me a copy of the Annex A/Rule 29 report which she had given to the judge last week, she remarked that everything *should* go through all right, her only concern being the lack of contact she has been allowed to have with Dom since our return home with José. Seeing as she only agrees to visit during working hours when Dom is at work, he has obviously missed most of our meetings. We had discussed this several times before, and she had agreed that providing she could see Dom twice with José, that should be sufficient. Dom took half-day holidays for those meetings, including a third visit for which Katrina herself arrived an hour and a half late. She had said this was sufficient, but now suddenly was saying it was not and could cause us a problem with our readoption. She added how concerned she was that Dom had not made more of an effort to be at home for her visits. I'm afraid I saw red, telling her in no uncertain terms that if she had needed to see him more and if her report reflected this, then she should have told us at the time rather than now when her visits were (hopefully) coming to an end.

Why she made the fuss, I have no idea. Her report was good and fair and did not mention any problems over Dom's lack of attendance at her many visits. We are grateful to her for giving us the good report, but quite why she had to harp on about it being a problem not seeing more of Dom, I really do not know.

There were a few comments in the report that did make us laugh, however, such as not having had the opportunity to interview José but getting the impression that he would like to remain with us. Her wording made it sound like we had prevented her from interviewing him. For goodness sake, José is only nineteen months old. He cannot even speak yet, so quite how she could have interviewed him, I really do not know.

Just how much more can we do to prove we are loving and committed parents to José?

We will certainly be glad when this is all over and we can banish social workers from our doorstep for good.

13 January 2009

I have just received some horrific and very tragic news that further demonstrates the dangers facing those living in Guatemala City. A number of years ago, Natasha, our adoption agent who is based in the United States and who arranged our adoption of José, adopted two children from Guatemala herself. One of them, by now a young man of eighteen years, was murdered on the streets of Guatemala

City last weekend. He was in the city to complete his education. Natasha posted a note online telling all the adoptive families she has helped over the years of his fate.

At the same time, she mentioned the murder of a twenty-four-year-old young man, the son of a director of one of the country's orphanages, who was gunned down a few days ago in the street with four others. In addition, a fifteen-year-old, known to Ana, our interpreter, was shot dead by a gang he had the misfortune to run into on his way to his aunt's house, and even a five-year-old, awaiting the final arrangements to be adopted, was murdered recently.

These deaths – whether they were poor innocent children or young adults – all occurred within the past week. In each case the victims just happened to be in the wrong place at the wrong time.

The news from Guatemala seems to get worse every day. It sounds like the country – or at least the capital, Guatemala City – is almost imploding on itself. I have read several reports recently that state that the violence in Guatemala is forcing people to live in a constant state of fear. In 2008 more than 6,200 people were murdered – close to seventeen deaths a day – and 10,000 cases of sexual violence were reported to the authorities. In the first three weeks of 2009, twenty-six women have already been murdered. Violence is particularly bad in Guatemala City, where many zones are strongholds of the *maras*, formed by young men previously deported from the US. Much of the violence is drug-related, but many innocent people get caught up in the crossfire and end up dead.

The impunity with which these criminals act is almost total. Natasha and her husband naturally want justice for their son's death, but they say that they know that in Guatemala this just will not happen.

In addition, the situation for many children in the country is also worsening. There are huge numbers of children in need of adoption, but since the introduction of the new adoption law a year ago, they have virtually no chance of finding a permanent home. Due to lack of funds, even Covenant House, the largest privately funded agency in the Americas providing shelter and other services to homeless, runaway and throwaway youths, is shutting down its refuge for street children in Guatemala.

It is not just for the love of our children that we, and many others I know, have adopted from Guatemala – it is also to save them from exactly the fate that befell Natasha's son. Certainly, as our adoption journey progressed, our adoption of a child from Guatemala became vital to us, not only so that we could have a baby of our own, but also to save at least one child from the poverty and other dangers of the country. How tragic that one of these adopted children should *still* fall victim to its horrendous rampant violence.

23 February 2009

This morning we received a copy of José's guardian's report from our solicitor. A copy has been sent to the judge to review prior to what we hope will be the final hearing for our adoption of José in this country in just two days' time.

We are relieved to see that she has written a great and highly complimentary report – so favourable, in fact, that our solicitor rang to say that we had obviously given her the full 'red-carpet treatment', and just what was our secret? In the end both Dom and I got on very well with Celia, who we found to be a breath of fresh air and full of sensible reasoning – rather unusual, in our experience, for an employee of social services. She is obviously very taken with José and, fortunately, satisfied with the care that we are giving him. She was particularly impressed by 'José's Story', the life-story book that I have written for José, and kindly commented that it was the best she had experienced in her career. As in the preparation course at the start of our adoption journey, I seem to have scored highest in my tasks involving cutting, pasting and preparing colourful children's pictures ... perhaps a career in a nursery school beckons?!

It is hard to believe that in just two days' time we could reach the end of our long road to adopt.

25 February 2009

At 10.30 this morning, at the Principal Registry of the Family Division (Families Court) in High Holborn, a district judge granted us an Adoption Order, thus legally confirming our adoption of José in the United Kingdom.

As the judge confirmed the order, Dom squeezed my hand and I struggled not to cry. We left the courtroom and I promptly burst into tears and had to rush into the ladies' to recover. Although we had always regarded this final part of the process – confirming José's adoption in the UK – as a mere formality, the relief was incredible.

All that remains now is a more informal hearing – a meeting between the judge and José. A legal adoption in this country requires the judge to meet the child being adopted. Most judges are happy to meet the child on the second/final hearing, but ours wished to do so on another separate occasion. This meeting is scheduled for mid-March.

12 March 2009

This morning Dom and I returned, this time with José, to the Principal Registry of the Family Division for the judge to meet José in order that the adoption is finalised in this country. My mother and Dom's parents accompanied us for this momentous occasion. The judge was friendly and in spite of being in the courtroom, the occasion was very informal. She allowed José to sit in her chair, beneath the royal crest, for photographs. She then handed us a certificate and rounded off the proceedings by saying: 'Congratulations José, you are now a member of the Bemrose family.' It was a great moment, and this time I even managed to stem my tears!

We then all went to the Rainforest Café for a celebratory lunch. José was beside himself with excitement throughout – during the train journey (his first); over the fuss that was made of him in the courtroom; at having lunch in a jungle (the Rainforest Café is a fantastic themed jungle restaurant, complete with moving animals and jungle sounds – perfect for children); and at having his favourite food (pizza and ice cream). He was even given a large cuddly chimpanzee as a present to round off the day. The centre of attention from start to finish, with both parents and his beloved grandparents lavishing attention on him throughout, he was totally spoiled and on cloud nine all day, but frankly, if we could not spoil him today of all days, when could we?

It is hard to believe that the long road to adopt is truly over. No more social workers; no more form-filling; no more uncertainty over José's future, or our future either.

Our journey to adopt has taken three years and five months. There have been many setbacks along the way, and it has been the most incredible emotional roller coaster of my life, but we have remained positive and focused on our goal throughout and today we received our reward: José is now legally our son and we are his parents, in British law as well as in Guatemalan law. Our dream has come true.

18

Reflections

March 2009

Over the last ten months, I have frequently paused as I look at our beautiful son and thought: *Our futures could have been so different.* I could so easily have missed out on the wonders of motherhood, and more importantly, what would have happened to José if we had not been allowed to complete our adoption? We were so close to being prevented – by the changes in the adoption laws of both Guatemala and Britain – from bringing José home. What struck me most about the transcripts that we received of the interview that Maria, José's birth mother, had with the British embassy was that her primary reason for relinquishing José was not for a *better* life for him, but to ensure his *survival*. This is a desire for the best for your child at its most elemental. What would have been his future if the change in adoption laws had prevented us from adopting him? Maria had already relinquished him and, like thousands of others, he would have had nowhere to go. At 'best' he would have been sent to an orphanage, but this is not a good option for the healthy development of any child. And the alternative? The streets of Guatemala City would have become his home. These thoughts terrify me. To think how close things came to this being the future for the boy who is now our son; how lucky we are – how lucky he is – that this was not the outcome. To us, he will always be our miracle child. And for José? He will have a loving family, a secure future, sufficient food and an education, but most importantly, he will, God willing, survive.

To those who disagree with intercountry adoption, believing that children should be brought up in the country of their origin and culture, I say this: Yes, in an ideal world I would agree that all children should remain in their native country, but the world is not ideal and if remaining in that country means a child is brought up in an orphanage, never knowing the love of parents and of family, or worse still, if remaining in one's native country means a child having to survive – or not, as the case may well be – on the streets, then surely a better option has to be for the child to be brought up in a secure family, even if that does mean the child has to leave his or her own country for one halfway round the world? If a country cannot protect and provide for its own children, then surely it cannot be wrong for people in other countries to love, protect and provide for them?

That said, I do believe that, having taken something so precious from a country, one does have a duty to give something back to that country. To this end, a charity called *Asofamilia* has been set up in Guatemala for the purpose of giving adoptive families the opportunity to sponsor the birth families of the children whom they have adopted. The charity provides education, health care and food packages for the birth family. This charity is currently looking for Maria, José's birth mother, to give her the option, should she so wish, of being sponsored by us. Hopefully this will go some way towards giving her a better life and ensuring any other children she has will survive. If we are unable to find her, then we will sponsor a child in Guatemala through one of the 'Sponsor a Child' organisations which operate worldwide. We feel it is the least we should do.

Our journey to adopt has been an interesting one. We have discovered a beautiful but impoverished country, Guatemala – a country ravaged by years of civil war, and currently still suffering from corruption, violence and poverty; a country full of cheerful people, breathtaking scenery and fascinating historical sites. We have met some wonderful, selfless people who dedicate their lives to helping the children of Guatemala, and we will never forget the amazing experiences we had in this stunning, colourful country.

When I look back on the three years and five months it took us to adopt – two years and seven months from starting the adoption journey to bringing José home, and a further ten months to complete the adoption in the UK – and reflect on the process, I am left with a great conflict of emotions.

On the one hand I feel complete happiness and true contentment with my life at present. I now have a beautiful, bonny son as well as a loving husband and I want for nothing. Friends told me to prepare myself for motherhood: 'It is hard'; 'You will miss your work'; 'Your time will never be yours again'; 'Gone is your social life', and so on. Yes, I suppose this is true, but to be honest, compared with the adoption process, looking after José is a piece of cake. I am pretty sure that I appreciate him so much – more than I could any biological child – because he was so very much harder to get. Even ten months on from the date he came home with us, the euphoria and the relief still seem almost tangible.

I feel immense gratitude towards all those who helped us in our journey to adopt. Gratitude to José's birth mother for giving him life and us a son – we will never forget her; gratitude to his foster family for their loving care of him during his first year – I am sure it is largely due to them that he came to us so confident, outgoing and well-adjusted; gratitude to our families and friends for supporting us along the way – we could not have made it without them; and gratitude to the lawyers, agency officials, bureaucrats and even the social workers – yes, I know I am a hypocrite – with whom we were involved, for without them we would not have our son.

I am grateful that we, Dom and I, managed to muster sufficient grit and determination to see this arduous process through to completion, and grateful too for my faith – my faith in God and also an optimistic faith that we would bring José home. Somehow I managed to cling to this faith throughout, and at times it was only this that kept me going.

I feel a very deep sadness at the desperate situation in which so many children in the UK, Guatemala and other countries throughout the world find themselves. I feel frustration and anger too at many aspects of the domestic and intercountry adoption systems which, for a variety of reasons, seem to conspire against uniting needy children with couples wanting to adopt.

Our experience of the bureaucratic system in this country is that it pays far too much attention to political correctness and far too little to the needs of children. The process seems almost designed to discourage potential adopters from adopting, whether domestically or from abroad. In the UK, too many potential adopters are rejected from the domestic adoption system on the basis of their ethnicity (white), their lifestyle (too middle class) or their age (too old). The practice of only placing children with adoptive parents of the same ethnicity desperately needs to be reviewed, otherwise too many children will continue to remain in care. According to a *Times Online* article on 2 April 2009 by Alice Thomson and Chloe Lambert entitled 'Too Old, Too Fat, Too Rich: Why Too Many People Can't Adopt a Child', last year UK adoptions fell to their lowest point in ten years – from 21,290 to 4,438, and these were mostly by relatives or step-parents. This number is woefully short of targets set by the government. Overseas, too, it seems that politics get in the way of what should be the main purpose of adoption – providing children with a loving family and a safe home.

The adoption system is too lengthy and too gruelling; with too many unnecessary hurdles and ingrained prejudices, so that too many couples and individuals who wish to offer a child a home are put off or find it impossible to see the adoption process through to the end. By the time we had completed our adoption in Guatemala and the readoption in the UK, we calculated that we had filled in thirty-seven forms, taking approximately eighty-one hours in total to complete, and that we had sat through forty-six hours of interviews with various social workers, plus twenty-nine hours of preparation courses and adoption talks. For the best part of two of the more than three years the adoption journey took us, I was spending at least five hours – and sometimes as much as twenty hours – a week working on our adoption. Much of this time was spent in research: on the country from which we would adopt, on the agency we would use, and on the ways in which we could overcome the many political and administrative hurdles that were put in our way. We travelled more than 32,600 miles with the four trips we took to Guatemala before we finally brought José home. The costs to adopt from overseas can be totally prohibitive for many people. For us, the cost of the entire process, including courses, agent and attorney fees and travel expenses for four trips to Guatemala, exceeded £30,000. We were lucky – we had some financial help from our families. Not everyone can afford this amount of time or cost. Is it any wonder there are still so many children out there in need of a home?

Would we adopt again? Yes. If Guatemala was still open to intercountry adoption we would almost certainly return to find a little brother for José, but the country is currently closed to overseas adoption, and Britain is closed to children being adopted from Guatemala. Who knows when the route will re-open? I will be too old by that time, of that I am certain.

I recently asked our local authority about our chances of adopting a second child, this time from the UK. Having adopted a child from Guatemala, we are now classed as a 'mixed-race' family, and as such this should, in theory, give us a greater chance of being matched with a child than we had initially when, as a white couple, we could only have been considered as a match for a white child. Our social worker told me that although in theory we should stand a greater chance, in practice we would only be considered for a child who was Guatemalan or was of 'uncertain ethnicity' but looked like he or she came from Central America. How ridiculous is that? What are our chances of finding a child matching these criteria in England? What would be so wrong in us having one child from Guatemala and another from, say, India or Africa? No, apparently this would not be considered. Furthermore, our social worker informs us that we would almost certainly not be accepted as adoptive parents for a white child now that we are a mixed-race family.

We had very little chance of domestically adopting a young child when we started; now, it seems, we have even less – virtually no – chance of adopting a young child within the UK as a sibling for José.

So, if we wish to adopt a second time, we would almost certainly need to look overseas again. With Guatemala now closed to inter-country adoption, we would need to research and get to know another country and its culture in the same way that we have Guatemala. That is a daunting prospect, particularly with our lives now full with caring for our son. Furthermore, there is an ever-dwindling pool of countries from which one can adopt and there are not many places we could consider.

If I am completely honest, I am not sure whether we have the emotional strength and the patience to go through the adoption process again. Whilst the social workers' interrogation and invol-vement in our lives is bad enough (we would have to go through the whole home-study and panel process once again), the end result is a reward worth the intrusion. No, it is not that that puts us off. It is primarily the possibility of failure. Suppose we put ourselves through the emotional roller coaster again and then the adoption falls through, due to the politics of the country or a change in the birth mother's decision to relinquish her child or other such reason? Do we have the emotional strength to survive the uncertainty, the set-backs and potential failures a second time? I am not sure that I do. Dom feels the same.

Furthermore, this time José would be involved. Even though he is still so young, social services would question him about his life with us; his feelings about having a sibling, and probably even film him at play. This is of great concern to us. José has been through enough already; we do not want to put him through any more stress and disruption. We do not want him to be subjected to being monitored. Although we would dearly love to have another child and a sibling for José, our one child – José – is everything and more than we could wish for. We feel so blessed, and on balance, we feel we should count these blessings and concentrate on José alone. He is reward enough.

As to my final thoughts ... The journey was long; the road was arduous and there were more lows than highs along the way, but there is certainly no doubt in our minds that it has been a truly worthwhile journey and a fascinating and interesting experience. We are now a family and José is a total joy and a delight to us. He is cheerful, affectionate and energetic, a healthy, happy little boy. We are so very lucky to have him, our little miracle, and we feel we are the luckiest parents in the world.

Epilogue

May 2010

On holiday in Suffolk – Exactly two years since José came home

Dawn

Dawn is breaking. I have slept well but am awake early. I can hear the wind whistling round the cottage; the rain beating at the windows. I slip out of bed and pull on jeans, a fleece and a waterproof, moving quietly so as not to wake Dom and José and creep outside, walking briskly to the seafront.

I stand looking out to sea. The waves are crashing round the pier and onto the beach; the wind is whipping at my face. It is raining heavier now. Within minutes I am drenched; Jeans clinging to my legs, hair plastering my face and still I stand. I cannot tear myself away from the beautiful, wild scene.

I am lucky. I have everything that I want in life. I have a kind, gentle and loving husband and a beautiful, happy, healthy, cheeky little boy. 'Thank You ... Thank You ... THANK YOU' I shout out loud. Crazy woman? Maybe! Crazy but happy. Very, very happy. Life is good.

Postscript

2010 / 2011: A campaign for change

I did not intend to publish a book about our adoption experiences. I wrote *Our Son from Afar* as a journal for therapeutic purposes, to help me get through the long months – years even – it took us to adopt; as a record of what I felt was such an extraordinary experience; and perhaps, in the future, as a reference for our son, José, to explain how we came to be his parents.

Then in 2009 Dom and I approached our local authority with a view to adopting a second child, this time domestically. Local authorities have long followed guidelines that suggest children should be placed with parents of the same ethnicity, a policy which has prevented many potential adopters from adopting and has seen many children of different ethnicities remain in care. It was largely due to our ethnicity that we had been turned away first time round – hence our journey to adopt intercountry rather than domestically – but now that we were a 'mixed race' family we were sure we would have more success. We were totally astounded by our local authority's response: not only would we not be considered suitable parents for a white child – as we now had a child of a different ethnicity in our home – but we also would not be considered for a child of any other ethnicity either. Our local authority would *only* consider us as potential adoptive parents if a Guatemalan child came onto their books. What were the chances of that?

I was once again reminded of the ridiculous hypocrisy of a system

211

that prevents white couples adopting children of a different ethnicity from within this country, but assesses and prepares them for adoption of a child from overseas; a child who clearly will not share their ethnicity.

Turned away for a second time on the grounds of ethnicity, I decided to take action. Whilst we could never regret, for a single moment, the route that led us to adopting our darling son, José, how ridiculous is a system that prevents so many couples from adopting in this country when there are so many children in need of permanent homes? *I would try and publish my journal to raise awareness of the problems with the British adoption system in the hope that changes – in particular regarding the ethnicity guidelines – would be made.* We are a multi-racial society so there is no justification to the obstruction of multi-racial families through adoption unless one also condemns mixed-race marriages.

Latest figures show that there were 64,400 children in care in March 2010, an increase of 6% on 2009, and yet children placed for adoption fell by 15% in 2009/2010. The average wait between a child being taken into care and adopted is two years and seven months, and at present ethnic minority children wait on average *three* times longer than white children to be adopted, with social workers often holding out for years to find adoptive parents who are an exact ethnic match (for the majority of couples or single persons who wish to adopt are white).

The system has to change. Ethnicity really should not be a barrier to a child finding a loving, stable and secure family.

At the same time I do believe it is very important that a child's native culture and heritage is not forgotten. Society has learnt from the mistakes of previous generations of trans-racial adopters: the method used in the 1950s and 1960s of denying original cultures and histories to adopted children is anathema to the adoption community today and, as taught on the adoption preparation course, adoptive parents nowadays understand the need to maintain and support ethnicity and culture.

Our Son from Afar was published in October 2010 and gained much media attention with interviews in the press, on television and on radio. The book and my subsequent campaign, led to my involvement with the Department of Education, which was in the process of reviewing the adoption laws. I was involved in round-table discussions with Tim Loughton MP, Parliamentary Under Secretary for Children and Families, regarding the drawing up of the new adoption guidelines, and, with input from numerous other adopters, I wrote a report for the Minister on the changes we believed were needed to the adoption system in this country.

The Adoption Guidance (First Revision 2011) was issued on 22 February 2011. It states: *'Any practice that effectively stops a child from being adopted because the child and prospective adopter do not share the same racial or cultural background is not child-centred and is unacceptable.'* (Source: Adoption Guidance – Introduction, Paragraph 5).

At the same time, the new guidance does draw attention to the importance of recognising a child's heritage and culture.

'All families should help children placed with them to understand and appreciate their background and culture. Where the child and prospective adopter do not share the same background, the prospective adopter will need flexible and creative support to be given by their agency. This should be in the form of education and training, not just simplistic advice, provided in a vacuum, on learning their children's cultural traditions or about the food/ cooking from their birth heritage. The support plan should consider how the child's understanding of their background and origin might be enhanced. This can include providing opportunities for children to meet others from similar backgrounds, and to practise their religion – both in a formal place of worship and in the home. Maintaining continuity of the heritage of their birth family is important to most children; it is a means of retaining knowledge of their identity and feeling that although they have left their birth family they have not abandoned important cultural, religious or linguistic values of their community. This will be of particular significance as they reach adulthood.' (Adoption Guidance – Chapter 4, Paragraph 8)

Success! Barriers preventing potential adopters from adopting children of different ethnicities have now been removed. Hopefully many of the thousands of children languishing in care in this country, unable to find adoptive homes because their local authorities cannot find an exact ethnic match, will now find permanent loving homes.

Dom and I have since been frequently asked if we will now adopt another child. It is not about that; the book and subsequent campaign were never about that. If the new adoption guidelines help one single child in care find a family and a permanent home, or to find that family more quickly then, frankly, mission accomplished.

Alex Bemrose – March 2011

Appendix 1

Timeline of Our Adoption Journey

2005

14 October:	Dom and I decide to adopt, and commence our research
November:	Attend Catholic adoption agency information evening about domestic adoption
December:	Attend Intercountry Adoption Consultation Day

2006

February:	Attend local authority information evening about domestic adoption
March/April:	Two interviews with a Catholic adoption agency about domestic adoption
May:	Initial interview with our local authority about intercountry adoption
July/August:	Intercountry Adoption Preparation Course
October–December:	Home study (9 x 3-hour interview sessions with social worker from local authority)

2007

March:	Home study confirmation meeting with another social worker
March:	Visit Guatemala for a holiday and 'recce'
27 March:	Adoption panel … *we pass!*
April:	Panel approval paperwork sent from local authority to DCSF
June:	Our dossier (adoption paperwork – including Certificate of Eligibility to adopt) leaves DCSF. It is sent to our notary for us to sign, then to the Foreign Office, the Guatemalan embassy in London, back to notary, before returning to DCSF and then to British embassy in Guatemala
19 July:	We receive a 'referral' offer from our adoption agency in USA: *'Baby boy, José, available for adoption in Guatemala'*
1 August:	'Referral' accepted (after confirmation meeting with Local Authority to review referral documents and meeting with notary to sign power of attorney)
October:	José's birth mother is interviewed by Family Court in Guatemala. Our adoption case then enters Family Court. José's birth mother is interviewed by British embassy in Guatemala. DNA tests are taken of José and his birth mother to ensure they are a match
November:	Our adoption case exits Family Court in Guatemala
13–17 November:	Guatemala. First visit trip: José stays with us for 3 days/2 nights (14–16 Nov) at Guatemala City Marriott Hotel
16 November:	Our adoption case enters PGN (Procuraduria General de la Nacion)

2008

11 February:	Adoption agency confirms our adoption case has been registered with CNA
20 February:	Receive notification of *previo* from PGN due to a problem with our paperwork, 13.5 weeks after entered PGN. Our case re-enters PGN two days later
29 February:	Adoption panel review in the UK
10–14 March:	Guatemala. Second visit trip: José stays with us for 4 days/3 nights (11-14 March) at Guatemala City Marriott Hotel
27 March:	*Out of PGN!* Our adoption case is approved and completed in Guatemala
April:	José's Guatemalan passport is issued. Our adoption case is filed with the British embassy in Guatemala. British embassy and DCSF approve entry clearance. British embassy in New York issues visa
5–14 May:	Guatemala. 'Pick-up' trip
5 May:	Flight from England to Guatemala
6 May:	'Family Day' – *José is handed over to us ... a family at last!* Collect José's passport and visa from British embassy in Guatemala
13 May:	Depart Guatemala (fly via Panama City and Madrid)
14 May:	Arrive London Heathrow – *home at last with José*
May–Jan 09:	Nine social worker visits, two social worker reviews and two guardian visits
November:	Adoption papers filed in the UK for adoption of José under British law

APPENDIX 1

2009

6 January: First hearing at Principal Registry of the
                      Family Division for adoption of José under
                      British law
25 February: Second hearing: Adoption Order confirmed.
                      José is now legally our son under both
                      British and Guatemalan law
12 March: Informal hearing with district judge to meet
                      José. *Adoption is completed.*

Appendix 2

Abbreviations

BAAF   British Association for Adoption and Fostering

Cafcass   Children and Family Court Advisory and Support Service

CNA   Consejo Nacional de Adopciones (Central Authority; set up January 2008)

CoE   Certificate of Eligibility (issued by the DCSF after one passes the adoption panel)

DCSF   Department for Children, Schools and Families (formerly the DfES)

DOS   U.S. Department of State

GFA   Guatemalan Families Association

IAC   Intercountry Adoption Centre

ICA   Intercountry adoption

OASIS   Overseas Adoption Support and Information Service

PAP   Prospective adoptive parent

PGN   Procuraduria General de la Nacion (Attorney General's Office)

Acknowledgements

Grateful thanks...

To my darling husband, Dom. We made it! At last we are a family.

To José, our beautiful little boy, who means everything to us. The trials and tribulations of the last few years paled into insignificance as soon as I held you in my arms. This story is for you.

To José's birth mother, for giving him life. You have made our dream come true and you will always have our eternal gratitude.

To José's foster family, for their wonderful loving care of José in his first year before we were able to bring him home. We could not have wished for our son to have a better start in life.

To our agent in America, her representative and interpreter in Guatemala, and our attorney in Guatemala, for finding José and handling the adoption arrangements in Guatemala. Thank you for so, so much.

To our families – the Lomax family (my mother, Tish Deacon, and my sisters, Susie O'Kelly and Kate Mackenzie) and the Bemrose family (Dom's parents, James and Frances, and his sisters, Penny Jekyll and Sasha Bemrose) – who supported us so incredibly throughout our journey to adopt, as they have supported us in everything in our lives. We cannot thank you enough for your support and prayers, and, of course, for keeping us relatively sane! A

221

special thanks also to my brother-in-law, Mark O'Kelly, for much time spent translating letters and documents from/into Spanish.

To Sarah (Puff) Hough, Kate Mackenzie (again) and Gopal Kutwaroo for being our referees and providing complimentary references to our social worker. Also thank you to Sarah Moy and Sarah Stilwell for being our legal witnesses.

To so many friends (too numerous to mention), clients, friends of friends, friends of our family, and members of the GFA, Guatemalafeliz, Guatadopt.com and OASIS, who supported us practically and emotionally throughout the long adoption process and who prayed for José's homecoming.

To those who offered me advice on how to get a book published – in particular, thank you Jane Rose, Sarah Stilwell (again) and Robert Gwyn Palmer for your invaluable help and guidance.

To Lord Howard of Lympne for kindly agreeing to read my book and for finding the time to write a foreword. I am most grateful.

To Rosemary Bennett (Social Affairs Correspondent, *The Times*) not only for writing about our adoption experiences and my book, but of more importance, for using them to illustrate some of the problems with the adoption system in this country. Your role in the campaign for changes to the adoption system should not be underestimated.

To Stevan Whitehead, Pippa Curtis and numerous other adopters for sharing with me their adoption experiences and opinions on the necessary changes to the domestic adoption system. Your help in preparing my Government report, regarding the proposed new adoption guidelines, was invaluable.

To my publishers, Book Guild Publishing, for your faith in my book, your advice regarding its publication and your excellent editorial assistance.